AN AFFAIR
OF THE HEART

AN AFFAIR OF THE HEART

A Spiritual Autobiography

یک مرد ساده

A Simple Man

Tavern Publications
ENCINITAS, CALIFORNIA

Tavern Publications
Encinitas, California

10 9 8 7 6 5 4 3 2
First Edition 2022
Printed in the United States of America

ISBN-13: 978-0-578-38981-3
Library of Congress PCN Number: 2022905164

Book design by Dynamic Book Design
www.DynamicBookDesign.com

From Hafez:
The great religions are ships,
Poets are lifeboats,
Every sane person I know has jumped overboard.

From Ibn Arabi:
I profess the religion of Love,
Wherever its caravan turns along the way,
That is the belief, the faith I keep.

From Farid ud-Din Attar:
I know Nothing,
I understand Nothing,
I am unaware of Myself,
I am in Love,
But with whom I do not know.

From Rumi:
I do not know who I am.
I am in astounded, lucid confusion.

From Rumi:
Come, we know a way from the seen to the Unseen,
A path from the house you've lived in for so long,
To a garden that will take your breath away.

I've created this book for the few Friends who love the feel of a "real" book, with pages turned slowly by hand. For as long as financial circumstance allows, this book will only be offered as a Gift, and only to those who ask. If I fall on hard times, it will only be offered at cost, for Love cannot be sold.

Within

Preface	9
In the Way of Introduction	19
A World of Joy and Sorrow	27
My Childhood Dance with Christianity	35
The Youthful Observer	43
Into the World	47
On Having Become Someone	57
A Preface on Teachers	65
The First Teacher of Significance	71
The Journey to The Kingdom of Heaven	81
The Inner Radiance	111
A Vision	121
A Period of Divine Madness	129
Mystical Experiences with My First Teacher	133
The Onset of Existential Reality	149
Disillusionment and Confusion	155
Wandering the Wilderness	161
The Second Teacher of Significance	167

An Affair of the Heart

Tough Crowd 177
Baba 181
The Third Teacher of Significance 205
The Dam Bursts 219
I Can't Feel Charles! 223
Emptiness Deepens 235
Little Monkey 241
The Sorrows of the World Pour In 249
The Reason to Live 255
Epilogue 263

Preface

*Oh God, not another
woo-woo[1] nutcake[2].*

This book reflects a simple man's spiritual journey and ongoing experience. Although much that's described may sometimes sound lofty and exalted, I dismiss the implied finality of notions such as "enlightenment" or "awakening", for my Experience has shown that it's unwise at best, and delusional at worst, to ever plant a flag and declare the summit.

While there have been profoundly transmuting milestones along The Way, in my experience there is no finality, here in manifest existence, to Endless Blossoming, Endless Deepening of Maturation, Endless Enlightening.

For me, at a ripe old age, it has come to this; that the measure of a human being is not in the commonly ascribed attributes of stature, worldly or spiritual, but the extent to which the lesser self, moved by fear, desire, and an ever-present sense of inner lack, has been

---

[1] One who holds unconventional beliefs with little or no scientific basis, in this case relating to spirituality and mysticism.
[2] Someone seen as eccentric or mad.

 An Affair of the Heart

subsumed by the Fullness, Completion, and Bliss inherent in our Essence.

About the Author

I'm a Western man. And as in any enculturation, there are good things about that, and bad. I consider myself rational and empirically-minded. But since early childhood my Heart has ached *about* something, and *for* Something; about the suffering inherent in manifest existence, and for… a mysterious Something Wonderful for which I had no description.

My feelings regarding religion and spirituality have always been conflicted. Some of us take refuge and find solace in belief and faith, others dismiss all that is not empirically verifiable, and others, still, are agnostic. Before 1981 I considered myself an agnostic; my lack of direct experience giving rise to skepticism, cynicism, and disbelief. After 1981, my stance would be better called "Not Knowing, and Full of Wonder". For in that year, skepticism, cynicism, and disbelief, though continuing in regard to religion, were vanquished regarding the Mystical Nature of reality.

The Heart

On the one hand my heart was broken at an early age by the cruelties of life, both natural and human, and I sought desperately for an adjunct to that reality that would somehow allow me to live within it and not die of a broken heart; an adjunct that was not, unfortunately, apparent in the "ordinary" reality I experienced. It was that desperation that moved me to investigate faith- and belief-

Preface

based religions, and philosophies. And fortunately, in spite of the inevitable disillusionments experienced along the Way, irrepressible Longing has proven to be an inherent and inextinguishable aspect of my Being. And if you're reading this, I suspect it is so with you.

The Mind

On the other hand I've always been rational and empirically-minded; a propensity that, in seeking to aid the heart in its quest, constrained it from unbridled emotionalism and the unexamined acceptance of unverifiable spiritual concepts, theories, and conjecture. This aspect of my Being had no use for belief or faith. It became, at a certain point in this Journey, not simply confused, disillusioned, and weary, but cynical and bitter regarding spirituality. It could not deny the direct Experiences I'd had, but simply could not abide wrapping them in interpretation, after the fact, or pouring them into the dogmas of this or that existing theology, however much affinity I might have with various aspects of a particular faith.

In the Balance

I have friends on both sides of this fence, from fierce empiricists, to those that I, myself, consider to be woo-woo. Likewise, I have friends who reside in various philosophical encampments, from nondualism to deism. The point of this preface is to make clear that in this book I am writing to neither.

Regarding my empirically-minded friends, little of what they'll read here is empirically verifiable – although one of the most

 An Affair of the Heart

outrageous experiences was, in fact, empirically verified[3]. If I wrote with empiricists in mind, I would be continually qualifying and apologizing for experiences they would likely dismiss as delusional at the worst, or simply of no significance according to their stance. I won't do that. I'll write of experiences as I experienced them, from my subjective perspective, striving to refrain from interpretation and theorizing, for which I have little use anymore. My empirical friends can make of it what they will. And I'm certain some will, in the end, consider me just another woo-woo nutcake.

Regarding my more spiritually-minded friends, I would ask them not to make more of any of this – and especially of "me" – than should be made. For however lofty and exalted some of these experiences may sound, I remain an imperfect, wounded, and in some ways, perhaps, broken man; a simple man.

Time's Running Out

I turned 72 the year of this writing, 2021. The average lifespan of men where I live, these days, is 78. Anyone reading this has a sense of how long seven years is; and it's not that long. Yes, yes, I know… I hear the chorus of voices saying, "Oh, but you could live to 90." And I certainly could. But the simple fact is that from the mid-sixties on, it's anyone's guess. And in the last several years, increasingly, I've heard of the passing away of so many among the cast of characters that have played upon the stage of my life; actors, musicians, those of varied notorieties, and closer to home, friends and acquaintances. However I look at it, it's the Winter of my life, and I'm increasingly aware of that fact throughout each

---
[3] See the chapter, "A Vision".

Preface

day, not simply now and then, as was the case in my sixties. But I only mention age here, in the context of this book, because standing shoulder-to-shoulder with the increased awareness of my mortality has been a voice that reminds me, gently but persistently, "If you don't write the book soon, you may never do so."

Write a Book? Why?

I'm writing because I want to offer hope that there is more to life than meets the eye; that the Mystical is real, and not a fairy tale born of delusional imagination or religious hysteria. I want to encourage consideration of the possibility that your Essence is an Experience of Ecstasy beyond words to express; the Kingdom of Heaven, within; the answer to every prayer ever uttered in all of Creation.

I want to suggest that the veils that obscure that Essence can be thinned, allowing that Light, that Richness, that Fullness and Warmth, that Causeless, Unconditional Love, to Shine into your manifest experience, not simply in moments of transient "spiritual" experience, but as an ever-present aspect of your ongoing, moment-to-moment Experience, Shining at the Heart of your Being as the Heart of your Being. I want to blow on the Ember in weary Hearts where it flickers tenuously.

Why Should You Believe What I've Written?

You shouldn't.

You should only trust what you Know in direct experience. All else is hearsay; concept, theory, and conjecture; the interpretations, by

An Affair of the Heart

others, of their experiences, after the fact. This book is about none of that. I don't present an interpretation of my past experiences or ongoing experience. I don't hold forth a theology, cosmology, or notion of "Truth". Any seeming assertions are merely questions, cloaked in possibility. Whatever commonalities may exist in our mutual experience, each of our Paths is unique. If I describe the Path I've taken, it isn't to inform, instruct, or suggest that Path to you, but only to Evoke Love and Longing, to ignite the Ember at the Heart of your Being.

As the saying goes, there are as many paths to God as there are souls on earth. Whatever your path may be, this book is written for those who, while reading the words written on these pages, experience a Touch, a Taste, the Fragrance of that which is written of; those with a Mystical Affinity and Resonance that cannot be understood or explained. You needn't believe a word I say, as long as you are "taken", and experience at the Heart of your Being a brightening of the Ember of Love, Longing, and Wonder; and for weary hearts, I pray, a quickening of wearied aspiration.

> Love[4] Shines,
> In the Wellspring of the Heart,
> For no one or anything in particular.
>
> Transcendent,
> It is simply our nature,
> Inherent in the Essence of Being.

---

[4] What is meant by "Love" would take a thousand inadequate words to describe. After reading this book, you'll understand that it's what I mean by The Inner Radiance.

Preface

And yet…
Everything and everyone, everywhere,
Is Lit by its Grace.

Immanent,
As the Compassionate Flow of Love,
Into manifest Creation.

This is how the Flame in one Heart,
Ignites, through its Light and Warmth,
The Ember in another.

Not only do I not expect you to believe what I will be telling you of my life and ongoing experience, I respect any skepticism you may have. For I am myself fiercely empirical and rational, even, and perhaps especially so, regarding my own direct experiences. However much affinity you may feel as you read, however much trust may accrue, I do not for a moment expect you to abandon discernment and discrimination, two of your greatest treasures.

I feel that in spiritual matters, more so than in any other affair of life, Honesty is the highest virtue, from which Humility naturally springs. I can only swear, for what it's worth, that I am being Honest in what I write, and am not exaggerating or seeking to make more of things – and especially of myself – than should be made.

I'm writing not to profit the "person" in any of the myriad ways that can happen. I have no desire to open a stall in the crowded spiritual marketplace. I write, in one regard, to offer hope to those who have abandoned the possibility that there is more to life than meets the eye, and feel that even if there is, it doesn't touch their life, and have no hope of its ever doing so.

An Affair of the Heart

Beloved, the scriptures caution us,
To avoid the dangerous trap,
Of mystical powers.

But please, Bestower of Grace,
Grant me just one power,
One Gift, not for myself…

To Ignite the Ember of Love,
In weary Hearts, drenched in despair,
Who arrive at the door of this Tavern.

Take a piece of Your Heart,
A gentle whisper of Your Grace,
And place it in mine.

Though this vessel is deemed,
By the lawyers of religion,
Unworthy, unfit, unclean.

Let Your Perfection, Shining,
In the midst of imperfection,
Be Proof to others "unworthy"…

Of Loves Unconditionality.

But I warn you, my Love,
If you Imbue me with such Love,
I will most surely misbehave…

Pouring Your Wine,
Into every cup held forth,
By those who notice its Fragrance…

Preface

>And ask, "Is Grace real?"
>
>If only I can Gift every drop,
>Before the legalists find and bind me,
>For spurning the Laws of Good and Evil…
>
>Filling every Heart,
>Everywhere,
>Now… and Forever.

In another regard, I write for those in whom the Ember is already alight.

>These words will only touch your Soul,
>If your Heart is already Pregnant.
>
>How will you know?
>
>The baby will Kick.

I write with the hope that you will feel the Honesty and Sincerity of this author, and become open to the possibility that what I'm saying is grounded in the fact of my Direct Experience, not in concept, theory, conjecture, intellectual conclusion, or in well-intended but misguided delusion. But my deepest hope, whether you believe me or not, is that my words carry, as I have seen them do for some, the Mystical Power to Illumine your Heart in Remembrance of "Something" Known, but forgotten.

>Longing is the remembrance,
>More ancient than ancient,
>Of something Known… but forgotten.

An Affair of the Heart

Forgotten, but alive within us,
As the Heart's Wordless Cry,
For something Known… but forgotten.

However hopeless we may be,
However faithless we become,
This Longing endures.

We may despair of religion,
But Longing endures,
For That which birthed all religions.

Longing for That which cannot be spoken;
Not that we cannot speak it,
But because… there simply are no words.

But… you Know it… don't you,
Reader of these failing words,
You Know, in your Sighing Heart…

That which was Known… but forgotten.

In the Way of Introduction

For those who find prose tedious, the following poem expresses the Essence of what is written in this book. For those who prefer a deeper dive, I offer the chapters that follow.

> What if, knowing little of the walled villages,
> Of religion, belief, faith, and philosophy,
> You experienced, one day, what seemed,
> When you considered it, after the fact,
> A loss of consciousness,
> The Vanishing of Everything from Awareness,
> Including yourself as the one aware, and yet…
>
> Awareness continued[5].

---

[5] An experience that I refer to as Nonexistent Existence; a term borrowed from Sufism. In Hinduism, it's samadhi. In some traditions, Union. In others…

 An Affair of the Heart

And what if the nature of that Awareness,
Pure and unsullied by space, time, and objects,
In which even you, the experiencer, had vanished,
Was so Ineffably Sublime that words did not exist,
To express its Ecstasy, its Rapture, its Perfection,
The Fulfillment of your Heart's Desire,
An Experience worthy of the phrase…

  The Kingdom of Heaven, within.

And what if you found yourself, thereafter,
Imbued always with a touch of that Heaven,
Felt as a Radiance in the Locus of your Heart,
Sometimes the ambient background of experience,
Sometimes flooding the foreground powerfully,
Ever available to the mind's Attention,
Ever available to the Heart's Remembrance…

A Wellspring, within, of Union's Dissolution and Ecstasy[6].

---

[6] An Experience of Being that I refer to as Illumination.

In the Way of Introduction

And what if you then entered the spiritual marketplace,
In search of someone, anyone, to explain the Mystery,
Wandering the rows of stalls, past the shouting hawkers,
Each declaring the "Truth", and decrying the others,
Until your eyes and ears could bear no more,
And your weary Heart pleaded with you to leave,
The pedantry, the arguments, the profaning of Love…

    And return to The Inner Radiance.

The simple Experience, not yet corrupted by the mind,
Beyond knowledge and understanding,
Not poured into the mold of another's interpretation,
Not bound by prescription, proscription, and dogma,
Not requiring you do this, or refrain from that,
Without cause, without condition, ever present,
A touch of Heaven, ever Shining Within…

    Fullness, Completion, and Bliss[7].

---

[7] The living Experience of Causeless, Unconditional Grace.

 An Affair of the Heart

And what if, in time, that Radiance in your Heart,
Like a Wellspring of Transmuting Love,
Vanquished the terrible pain of yourself,
Leaving intact all that you had taken yourself to be,
But stealing from your experience, the felt sense of "you[8]",
That very felt sense that had vanished one fateful day,
Long ago in time, when time and all things Vanished…

And only Nonexistent Existence remained.

And what if, the mind no longer in desperate need,
You returned to the spiritual marketplace,
Moved now only by Curiosity, Wonder, and Love,
And found yourself Dancing past the stalls,
Stealing this jewel from here, that jewel from there,
Until, your satchel full to overflowing,
You Thanked them all, Rested again…

In The Inner Radiance.

---

[8] An Experience I refer to as Liberation.

In the Way of Introduction

And what if, moved by Love and Compassion,
You declared to any who might ask,
This Beautiful Presence,
This Shining Radiance,
This Exquisite Rapture,
This Fulfillment of the Heart's desire,
The Divine Thief that has stolen 'me'…

I will call it God,
I will call it Brahman,
I will call it The Beloved,
I will call it The Holy Spirit,
I will call it Emptiness that is Full,
I will call it The Inner Light,
I will call it The Unnameable…

        I will call it Love[9].

And what if you were told, one day,
To your surprise and amazement,
By some among your Friends,
That the ember within their Hearts,
Ignited, to their Delight and Inspiration,
In moments of Relationship with you,
Shining ever more Brightly, over time…

---

[9] In truth there is no word for This.

 An Affair of the Heart

Until they found themselves, in time,
Imbued always with the touch of Heaven,
Felt as a Radiance in the Locus of their Heart,
Sometimes the ambient background of experience,
Sometimes flooding the foreground, powerfully,
Ever available to their mind's Attention,
Ever available to their Heart's Remembrance…

I will call it… a reason to live[10].

And what if you found, in the course of your long life,
No finality in the stations[11] come to along The Way,
No summit to declare, no flag to be planted,
And that however Profound the milestones come to,
More should not be made of them than should be made,
Each being merely a Tavern, a Station arrived at,
Another Garden of Grace discovered…

On a Journey of… Endless Enlightening.

---

[10] Having nothing to do with the egoic "person."
[11] A Sufi term referring not to transient experience, but enduring transmutation.

In the Way of Introduction

All these words I have written of Liberation and Illumination,
May have given you the illusion that I have my bearings,
And an understanding of all that's happened,
And all that is to unfold in time,
When I am simply adrift,
Without compass,
Rudderless,
Here…

In this Great Mystery.

 An Affair of the Heart

A World of Joy and Sorrow

*Joy and sorrow dance together, here,
One never letting go of the others' hands.*

We are born into an experience of opposites, of extreme polarities and everything in between. In our manifest existence, Heaven and hell are here for us, depending both on circumstances, our state of mind and, I feel, the nature of our Being. For there are those whose Hearts remain alight in the midst of hellish conditions, and those who, having everything deemed desirable in life, cannot bear to live a moment longer.

>Joy and Sorrow dance together here,
>One never letting go of the others hands,
>As the Divine Musician orchestrates,
>Allowing each their place upon the floor.
>
>An Incomprehensible Mystery, it seems to me.
>
>Sorrow is not denied its mournful turning,
>Nor Joy alone allowed its whirling delight,
>For these two dancing together, as one,
>Are inherent in the Ecstasy beyond dualities.

 An Affair of the Heart

> For a time I danced alone with Joy and Sorrow,
> But one day turned, to Sway in The Beloved's arms.
> Then, taking up the Instrument of my Soul,
> I returned to the floor, to Play while Dancing.
>
> Laughing and Crying as I had before,
> But Surrounded, now, by Her Perfume,
> Transcendent and Immanent, both at once,
> Dancing imperfectly, with my Perfect Partner.

The Great Sorrow

Although born into a loving family in a time of great prosperity and peace where I never knew hunger, deprivation, or the horrors of war, my Heart was broken, nonetheless, early in life, as I discovered those aspects of manifest existence, born of both Nature and humankind, which cause all Gentle Hearts to recoil in horror, sorrow, and rage. Later in my life I would refer to this horror, sorrow, and rage as *The Great Sorrow*. For although horror and rage arose in response to transient circumstances, sorrow seemed to linger perennially.

The revelation of life's more brutal aspects comes to us all, of course, and most find ways to carry on, keeping The Great Sorrow at bay, more or less successfully. But some of us, for reasons beyond my understanding – perhaps simply due to our nature – carry always within us an awareness of, and a felt sense of the suffering in this world; sometimes predominantly in the foreground, other times as a subtle ambience in the background; but ever present, ebbing and flowing.

Within The Great Sorrow, rage cried out, "No! Stop!" while Sorrow

A World of Joy and Sorrow

cried out, "No! This can't be all there is!" These two became ever-present aspects of my experience of life; one enraged and wanting to fight, the other sobbing hopelessly. At first Sorrow cried out in a desperate hope for something other than the harsh nature of outer reality; the cruelties of humankind and Nature, and all manner of sufferings that ensued. Later in life, Sorrow would also come to cry out for something other than the inner feeling of embodied separateness and isolation; something other than the feeling of myself that I had come to identify with, bound in endless self-referencing, self-judgment, and an exhausting concern for stature and standing; something other than all of those aspects of existence too numerous to grasp or enumerate, that caused my Being to contract into a knot of Spiritual Unhappiness.

There is an event of my early childhood that's archetypal of my introduction to the harsh realities of life. I was eight years old and in the third grade when Mom took me to see the movie, Bambi. I hadn't had much exposure to the world at large, beyond Mom, Dad, home, and those few years of schooling. I knew little of the natural world, and my experiences in school had only brought the beginnings of insight into human nature. But that was all about to change.

Sitting in the theater, I was enthralled at first, falling in love with Bambi, Thumper, Flower, and the other creatures. The forest was gorgeous; an idyllic paradise for those sweet beings to frolic in. The tender affection of Bambi's mother reminded me of my own Mom, and I saw in the various creatures, fond reflections of my schoolmates.

But soon enough, I was horrified, and filled with the first inklings of sorrow and rage. For I was shown that there were humans

 An Affair of the Heart

in this world who sought to kill the creatures, and in fact killed Bambi's Mom, and my Heart broke. I saw fire, which burned the beautiful forest and its animals in torturous deaths, and my Heart broke. Seeing the terror in their eyes as they fled, my Heart broke in empathy, and cried, "No! Stop!" and "No! This can't be all there is!" I saw wolves, snarling, vicious, and menacing, surrounding Bambi's girlfriend, the doe, Faline, reminiscent of the bullies at school, and my Heart broke.

It was not simply the hunters who seemed in my simplistic young mind to be cruel, even demonic. For impersonal Nature, through the fire, had shown itself to be unforgivably cruel. The archetype of the hunters and the snarling wolves were unambiguous targets of my rage. But in Nature there was no "who", in those early years, toward which I could focus my ire. Only slightly later, when I more clearly understood Christianity's notions of a creator God whose "Divine Plan" included this cruelty and suffering, would my rage find a target.

Heartbreaking Beauty

Of course life is not all darkness, and I went on to experience the Breathtaking Beauty of Nature, and to recognize within humanity, and myself, the better angels of our nature. I experienced the ecstasy of life, as well as the agony. And as in all lives, there were times in the ebb and flow when Joy would predominate and The Great Sorrow was diminished to a distant ambiance. But always, however diminished, The Great Sorrow was present, there in the mix, even in moments of joy; a melancholic spice, ever present in

A World of Joy and Sorrow

the Masala[12] of my moment-to-moment experience.

To this day my experience is – to use a confounding term for a confounding experience – Heartbreakingly Beautiful. For contradictory as it may sound, as The Great Sorrow deepened over time, so did an inexplicable Richness of Heart born of that Sorrow's coexistence with the Exquisite Beauty of this world and the inner Radiance of Love and Compassion that is inherent within us all; a Richness and Depth that would not be possible if either polarity was excluded.

And looking back I recall – although it was not apparent at the time – that in those moments when this Exquisite Heartbreaking Beauty was experienced with intensity, or in moments when Longing for the mysterious Something Wonderful, born of "No! This can't be all there is!" overwhelmed me, there was also present the first ever-so-subtle Fragrance of Bliss[13], the Perfume of The Beloved, the nature of our Essence.

> There is a Beautiful Sorrow.
> How can I ever explain?
>
> So Beautiful...
> I would never dream to "transcend".
>
> A Sorrow Illumined by that Love,
> Which is beyond Joy and Sorrow.
>
> So Beautiful...
> I would never dream to "transcend".

---
[12] A spice mix in East Indian cuisine.
[13] The Experience of the Soul's Ecstasy, diminished by its arising in manifest experience, but its source, unmistakable.

An Affair of the Heart

Born of the BitterSweet Transience,
Of our existence in this ephemeral Dream.

So Beautiful… so Terrible…
I would never dream to transcend.

Lovers of the Absolute would leave this world,
And vanish in formless transcendence.

I Vanished in that Transcendent Heaven,
And returned, not transcendent, but…

Illumined with Love's Immanence.

Love for this Wondrous World,
Of Heaven, and of Hell.

So Beautiful… so Terrible…
I would never dream to transcend.

I have drowned in Her Formless Embrace,
And awakened again on the shores of Duality.

Drenched in the Water of Her Presence,
Here, in the land of Joy and Sorrow.

Her Wine Intoxicates every Heartbeat,
Here, in The Tavern of The Beloved.

Her Fragrance Blesses every breath,
Here, in Her Secret Garden.

This life, so Beautiful… so Terrible…
I would never dream to transcend.

A World of Joy and Sorrow

BitterSweet tears of Ecstasy and Agony,
Fall for this Beautiful… Terrible World…

I would never dream to transcend.

 An Affair of the Heart

My Childhood Dance with Christianity

The Sea will be the Sea,
Whatever the drop's philosophy.
-Attar of Nishapur

The Conflict of Love and Theology

Born in 1949 in post-WWII America, the religion I was introduced to as a child was, of course, Christianity. I started Sunday School when I wasn't yet three years old at a non-denominational Protestant church. And although I have few memories of early youth, there are a few which point to an intense spiritual Longing early on.

As I came to understand the Christian faith more deeply, it became clear that my stance was Mystical, not doctrinal, driven by Longing born of The Great Sorrow and the cry, "No! This can't be all there is!!" I suspect this Mystical perspective is true of most children.

 An Affair of the Heart

However much my parents loved me, teachers encouraged me, or friends in school showed kindness, the Great Sorrow stood always nearby in the shadows of awareness, reminding me that however peaceful and pleasant my circumstance, somewhere, in each moment, there were cruelties taking place, man-made or natural, and someone or something was suffering as a consequence – someone or something I might love deeply, if only I knew them; someone or something that was screaming, "No!"

I was never quite sure about "God". In all my time as a Christian, I was at odds with the notion of a Being whose Love was conditional, with the notion of judgment and punishment, heaven and hell, and with Abrahamic theology in general. In fact, I'm not certain any Christian sect would have considered me a Christian. As time passed, I became fiercely defiant of an anthropomorphized God who would require the torturous death of his son as a sacrifice.

As I learned more, over time, so much of Christian theology seemed to me the invention of simple-minded primitives, or ancient leaders seeking to manage the lesser instincts of restive populations. Nor did I give much credence to descriptions of what might come after death, for they could not be proven, and were, for me, even at an early age, merely theories. I was concerned with life, here and now; with how to live, how to not be consumed by The Great Sorrow, and where to find the answer to, "No! This can't be all there is!"

As many Christians do, I simply compartmentalized the theological aspects I found distasteful, and held fast to a faith-based belief in the Mystical Existence of Jesus as an incarnation (now disincarnate, but still Alive) of all that was the antithesis of the lesser aspects of human nature; an Absolutely Selfless Being of Pure, Unconditional

My Childhood Dance with Christianity

Love and Compassion, whose only agenda in existing was to Bless. My hope was that in relationship with such a Being, he would, in his Infinite Compassion, reveal to me the answer to, "This can't be all there is!"

Decades later, looking back at that time, I would come to see that it wasn't the Being of Jesus that I Loved, but the qualities of Selflessness, Love, and Compassion that he embodied in my imagination. If a rock had exhibited those qualities, I would have Loved the rock. If I'd been a Muslim, I would have sought God as The Merciful, The Compassionate, The Beautiful, The Beloved. But in my youth, I knew nothing of other faiths.

Resonances

Even in my youth what I took to be Jesus' Living Presence was not simply an intellectual abstraction or the product of overly imaginative emotionality, but a reality of direct experience. What I would call, much later in life, The Inner Radiance, was not then a constant, or as viscerally, powerfully present as it would later become. It was a transient Sweetness and Richness of Heart, arising in moments of absorption in deep Longing. In those moments it seemed that the Radiance was a response to my Longing, bestowed by Jesus; the Presence of the Holy Spirit. It never occurred to me, then, that it might be the Nature of my own Essence. But however I may have interpreted and related to the Experience at that time, looking back I see that it contained the first subtle inklings of The Inner Radiance; a Great Peace, a Comforting Warmth, an Ecstatic Fullness of Heart, the embrace of Causeless, Unconditional Love and, in a way that had nothing to do with the accumulation of knowledge, a Teacher and a Teaching.

 An Affair of the Heart

Although so many aspects of Christianity put me off, there was an excitement of recognition when I discovered the Biblical passage regarding the Holy Spirit; "But the Comforter, which is the Holy Spirit, whom the Father will send in my name, shall teach you all things, and bring all things to your remembrance." Was the Radiance in my Heart Jesus, or this Holy Spirit, or... what? Were they somehow one, as the scriptures said? The religionist in me wondered with hope and faith, while the empiricist curled his lip in disdain. For whatever I might conclude would be nothing more than unprovable conjecture.

Whatever that Presence might be, I was resonant with the Pentecostal sects' assertion of the existence, not simply in ancient times, but today, of a Mysterious Living Presence they deemed the Holy Spirit, that could be experienced directly by a Heart filled with Longing. For this was how I interpreted, at that time, my own experience of The Inner Radiance. I would later be delighted when I also found this emphasis on direct experience in the Mystical traditions of various other faiths; however much I may have been at odds with their theologies.

How could I believe in a Mystical Jesus, in a Holy Spirit, but dismiss almost the entire theological context in which those were presented? It was lunacy, I knew, even then. And the schism between theology and my Heart's Desire was ever-present in my experience of and relationship with Christianity. But such is the case with so many whose true religion, perhaps as yet undiscovered by them, is Love. My dismissal of theology aside, I was, at this point in my early life a religionist, for my stance rested, if not on belief, on a most desperate, tenuous, and seemingly futile faith and hope.

My Childhood Dance with Christianity

Recollections

The first clear recollection of my early spiritual nature is from age eight, when for several Wednesday afternoons I gathered a small group of friends together under the awning of our mobile home in South Carolina, where I read from the Bible, and we talked about Jesus. It seems implausible to me, looking back. But it happened.

Another incident at eight years old was when my parents invited several of their friends over for drinks. In our mobile home, my bedroom was separated from the living room only by a thin, sliding door. In the course of the evening alcohol loosened the constraints of behavior, and at one point I overheard what seemed to me to be crassness expressed by one of the men toward the woman who had accompanied him. I had the sense, quite possibly misconstrued, that the woman had been hurt by what I heard as an unloving and unkind series of remarks. Whether misconstruing and misguided or not, I began crying in a mixture of sadness and anger, and opening the sliding door, tears streaming, walked into the living room and chided, "How can you talk to her that way?! Don't you love her?!" My Dad walked me back into my room and tucked me in again. I can't remember what he may have said.

Perhaps I was simply a little religious prig[14]. Whatever the case, overhearing what I felt to be demeaning unkindness, The Great Sorrow had overwhelmed me. This was the same year that Mom had taken me to see the movie Bambi, and perhaps I was still awash in the shock and horror of what I had seen there. In my adult life, it should be noted, I behaved, at times, in ways my childhood self would have deemed crass and debased, while an older, less

---

[14] A self-righteously moralistic person who behaves as if superior to others.

 An Affair of the Heart

dogmatically black-and-white self would deem them simply as expressing a lust for life.

When I was eleven, we lived in Orange, Texas; the last stop in what had been many years of perpetual relocations, after which we would return to San Diego. I'd made a little altar in my bedroom; a remnant of burgundy velvet I'd somehow come across, covering a small table, with a crucifix upon it – in spite of my dismissal of the notion that Jesus had suffered for our sins. That same year I wrote in Mom's Baby Book[15], under ambitions, "I want to be a minister."

But I didn't want to be a minister in the commonly understood sense. I wanted, with all my heart and soul to be one of Jesus' disciples, imbued, as I felt they had been, with a Mystical Gift to Heal and Bless. I wanted to be a Mystic in the most Profoundly Beautiful sense of the word. I wanted to be Healed and Blessed myself, so that I might be useful in Healing and Blessing others, easing The Great Sorrow within them. I wanted to be filled with the Divine Presence in every moment; a Presence which at that time came only fleetingly in rare moments of contemplation or prayer, as a faint, distant Radiance, barely palpable.

When I'd read the Biblical story of the man to whom Jesus had said, "Come, follow me," who had replied that he couldn't, because of his worldly responsibilities, I would cry inwardly, "Ask me! Ask me!" But of course, later in life, I, too, would not follow, and would even, at one point, bid a loving farewell to Jesus, and to Christianity. But if he existed, I thought, and was indeed a Divine Locus of Selflessness, Loving Kindness, and Compassion as I'd held him to be, then no matter my farewell, he would never abandon me.

---

[15] A book in which Mom logged the events of my youth and kept photos.

My Childhood Dance with Christianity

I have studied the lives of the great saints,
Perfected in virtue and "spiritual" qualities…

And I am not one of those.

I have admired those with will and discipline,
Who struggle and strive so fiercely…

And I am not one of those.

I have listened to diamond-like articulations,
From those blessed with eloquence of mind…

And I am not one of those.

I have known those whose hearts are warmed,
By Faith and Hope, alive and shining…

And I am not one of those.

If Grace had not showered upon this weary Soul,
Simply because, I Am…

If Love had not Blossomed in this aching Heart,
Simply because, I Am…

I would have been lost, forever, beyond all hope,
And this life made a living Hell.

For I did naught in the way of perfecting,
Or making "worthy" this broken vessel…

But only Cried out for Love, Unconditional.

An Affair of the Heart

And if that Love without condition had not come,
Simply because I Am…

I would surely have Cried myself to death.

The Youthful Observer

*How odd,
these humans.*

The Wandering Years

My Dad was in the Navy, and from age seven to eleven (grades 2-6 in elementary school) mine was a life of continuous relocations, never finishing a year in one school. We moved from San Diego, California, to Michigan, then South Carolina, Rhode Island, Illinois, Texas, then home again to San Diego.

For those five years, I was a perpetual stranger, ever the new kid. If I wasn't introverted and introspective by nature, those circumstances certainly contributed to my becoming so. There was never enough time in any location to become socialized in the way that constancy allows, to move deeply into the human interactions and melodramas that I could only watch play out in school after school; interactions that shape, in those early years, so much of our young persona. I never felt a sense of belonging, of being "a part of." In the few instances where I began to form friendships with some depth, they were soon cut short.

 An Affair of the Heart

And so, from my sequestered perspective, I observed as a bystander, and in the manner of a young person, studied human nature. In my peers at school I noted archetypal personas. Among others, there was the quiet one, withdrawn; the friendly, outgoing one; the insecure one, tentative and sometimes defensive; the needy attention seeker; the kind, caring one; the petulant one, given to sulking and pouting; the imperious know-it-all; and of course, the bully. Some of the characters from Bambi were there, moving in real life as humans.

Not yet moved by life to inquire, "Who am I?", I studied, instead, the "who" of others, assiduously. Throughout this period of wandering and for a time after settling back in San Diego, I remained wrapt in this studied fascination of human nature in others. For in all those years of wandering, I had become established in a kind of aloof exceptionalism, having come to feel myself as "not one of them".

During this nomadic period I took refuge and found a sense of personal stature in academia, especially the study of history and the humanities. At one point, still quite young, I could recite, at a high-level, a chronological history of civilization from Ur of the Chaldees to the fall of Rome. I was enraptured of all things ancient; the further back, the more mystified I became. When I reached the Industrial Revolution in my historical studies, I lost all interest. For it seemed the Mysticism I'd imagined as being present up until that time had in that era vanished from the world. I viewed history from the Industrial Revolution to the modern era with a deep disdain and contempt.

When we returned to San Diego late in 1961, I was 11 years old and in 6th grade. It was then that my teacher suggested I be put up a grade[16], but my parents refused, fearing the notoriously rough nature of the junior high school I would have been attending. They didn't consult me about this, and when I found out about their denial, it broke my spirit. For being put up a grade is, for an academic kid, equivalent to the medal of honor. After discovering this denial – which, in retrospect, showed wisdom on the part of my parents – I lost interest in all studies except my continuing fascination with history and the humanities. I would eventually pass high school with minimum grades in all other classes. In fact, I was given a D- in "remedial" math, as a kindness from that teacher, so that I could graduate, when in fact I had failed even that level.

Joining the Party

It would not be until 1965, when I was 15 and a sophomore in High School, that I would make a conscious decision, no doubt driven by adolescent hormones, to no longer be the observer, the student of humanity, but to dive into the human experience with all my heart. I made friends, joined a band (a true garage band), and had a girlfriend with whom I fell madly in love. The cloistered monk within me – for that is, in a certain sense, how I had come to perceive myself – was locked away in his cell.

This sense of a "spiritual" self and a "worldly" self, had formed through my embrace of Christianity, early in my youth. And although the monk had been locked away when I chose to enter the human experience, his voice – both his Wisdom and his Ignorance – would whisper to me throughout my journey in the world, causing

---

[16] This wasn't because I was exceptionally bright, but because my sequestered life during those years of wandering had driven me to academia, and because the Eastern schools I'd attended were rigorous.

An Affair of the Heart

both an enrichment of experience and a good deal of grief. For however much insight, kindness, compassion, and unconditional Love there was in my stance toward others, there was, regarding myself, a bitter dose of self-judgment and condemnation, born of the lesser aspects of Christianity; lesser aspects I would eventually find in other religions of the same ilk.

Into the World

Had I known there was such a huge pit,
In which to throw one's sins,
I would have committed many more.
    -Girish Chandra Ghosh

We're foolish when we ask anything to last.
But surely... we're still more foolish not to take
delight in it while we have it.
-W. Somerset Maugham, *The Razor's Edge*

In 1965, during my sophomore year of High School, when I was 15 years old, I took up the guitar. My Dad had bought me a cheap guitar with strings so far off the neck, and of such a thick gauge, that no human alive could play it without pain. My progress was so hindered that by my Junior year I had switched to keyboards, and had my first paying job playing in a band. The wave of the '60s cultural and musical revolution was breaking over America, and it was an auspicious time to become a musician. The momentum of that cultural tsunami would carry me through a 16 year career, until it washed me up, weary and disheartened, onto the shores of 1981, 31 years old. I hadn't really chosen music as a career, but had

 An Affair of the Heart

simply fallen into it. And the place in time of its beginning during the '60s had made lingering in that lifestyle irresistible.

In those years as a musician, the dance of Joy and Sorrow whirled with an intensity few other lifestyles would have afforded. No sooner had I consciously emerged from my inner solitude, than I was swept away into one of the most intense social whirlwinds possible at that time. In those years, in that profession, I learned more about human nature, in others and in myself, more about life and love, both selfish and selfless, conditional and unconditional, than I could have imagined.

Existential Fear

Although life as a musician was one of uncommon richness, intensity, and vibrancy, it was an extremely difficult life in the way of financial insecurity. For the most part, through those 17 years, I lived paycheck to paycheck, with brief periods of tenuous security during a few of the longer engagements. But even those extended engagements provided only a meager existence. And so, a new spice of Existential Fear was added to the Masala of moment-to-moment experience, a fear that co-existed with The Great Sorrow and the Joys of life that I openheartedly embraced. Another chapter could have been written to the story of Bambi, in which the availability of food became uncertain for the woodland creatures, and they lived in near constant anxiety and fear.

Into the World

A Fateful Prophesy

When I was 19, only a couple of years out of High School and at the beginning of my musical career, the insecurity of that lifestyle had already become overwhelming. Lying in bed one night I found myself so unable to control the onslaught of fear and insecurity, fused as it was with The Great Sorrow, that I wondered at my ability to carry on, and without knowing how accurate it would turn out to be, a thought came to me that would prove to be prophetic.

I thought to myself that it seemed altogether likely that by the age of 30 I might be dead by my own hand, unable to bear existence any longer. Or worse, still, I might be institutionalized and unable to take my life. But another thought also occurred to me; a third option that I dismissed cynically as foolish optimism. There was the highly unlikely possibility that something might happen in my life – something that, laying there in bed that night, I couldn't imagine – that would change my life and enable me to carry on. I could not have known, then, that at 31 something would occur; something that would allow me not only to carry on, but do so with an Illumined Heart.

Decades later I would look back and understand that I never wanted to die. For I have always loved this life of Joy and Sorrow, and this Beautiful, Terrible world. I simply didn't want to continue living in the state of being I was experiencing at that time. So much would be revealed in the future, regarding states of mind.

As it turned out, full of fear and insecurity, I went on to be relatively successful at staying employed, with some notable downtimes in which a dear friend would save my life by offering his floor and a sleeping bag until I could get back on my feet. Without his friendship, I've no idea what would have become of me, or how I would have survived those times of destitution.

A Farewell to Jesus

By the time I grew into adolescence, I had given up any hope of fitting into formalized, structured Christianity, and in 1972, 22 years old, I had a heartfelt talk with Jesus in which I said a tearful goodbye, not only to the theology of Christianity, but to the tattered faith I'd held in him. I had been too conflicted, for too long, about too many aspects of that religion. If the Jesus I held in my Heart existed, he would understand. If not, so be it. Summoning courage, I pushed open the gate of the walled village of Christianity, and walked into the Spiritual Wilderness in search of the Experience I Longed for, of Unconditional Love, unwrapped in the requirements of theology.

> Far from the village…
> Road vanished into path…
> Path vanished into hillside…
> Hillside vanished into Vastness…
> The Known vanished into… Wonder.
> -The author

I could not deny the transient experiences of the strange Inner Radiance I'd felt in relationship with thoughts of Jesus or in moments of contemplation and prayer; a Radiance I'd not felt at any other times in my life. But it seemed to me that if that Radiance abandoned me upon my leaving Christianity, it was not what I'd sought; an experience of Fullness, Completion, and Bliss, unbounded by any conditionality whatsoever.

Into the World

> The great religions are ships,
> Poets are lifeboats,
> Every sane person I know
> Has jumped overboard.
> -Hafez

The Wilderness Way that I followed from that day on proved difficult, for there was much in tradition that benefited, comforted, and nurtured, however much, in other ways, it hindered and hobbled. In the decades to come, as I visited and lingered for a time in the walled villages of other faiths, it was Love, Longing, and Wonder that sustained me, not faith in the unprovable, or belief in a theory.

The Great Sorrow, and the Wellspring of Longing it birthed continued to move me in my search, no matter how disillusioned or disheartened I became, again and again, along the Way. I would realize later in life that The Great Sorrow, however painful, was a Blessing. It was an Angel, moving me, through Unbearable Longing, to persevere; woven, as it had become, into the fabric of my Being.

> Pray for thirst, not water.
> -Rumi

My Introduction to Eastern Philosophies

Few of my generation could avoid exposure to Eastern spirituality during the '60s and early '70s. It played a significant part in the social revolution that swept through America. But in spite of its popularization, my engagement had remained shallow. In 1972, the same year that I said a formal goodbye to Christianity, I discovered the book *Be Here Now*, by Ram Dass. Reading that book was

   An Affair of the Heart

the first time I actually dipped my toes into the ocean of Eastern spirituality, and I was captivated and mystified by it all, especially the notion of "enlightenment"; of coming into what I hoped might be the Christ-like state of being I held so dear.

Being generally unable to focus for extended periods, I've never been much of a reader, but driven by Longing and fascination I went on to read several of the spiritual books that were popular in that era, from Alan Watts to Yogananda's *Autobiography of a Yogi*. Doing so, I discovered that the word enlightenment had different meanings in different traditions. Like a child wandering alone through the spiritual marketplace, I soon became confused and disheartened.

My infatuation with Eastern Philosophy was also tinged by my inability to have faith in the unprovable. My tenuous assent to faith had been mortally wounded in my time as a Christian, replaced by an ever more ferocious empiricism and skepticism. As much as my heart longed for the fantastical stories I'd read of in various religions to be true, my mind could no longer surrender to belief in hearsay, however marvelous or miraculous. And in spite of the desperate Longing which, it seemed, could not be extinguished by discouragement or doubt, I held, for many years to come, a deep-rooted suspicion that the mystical experiences of which I'd read were nothing more than the delusional imaginings of hysterical religionists. That stance would change many years later, in November of 1981. But... I'm getting ahead of myself.

Into the World

Playing by Heart

Being self-taught and unable to read music, I "played by ear", as they say. The critiques of the self-taught are well known, and I accede to their accuracy. If you do not learn to play properly – using the right fingering techniques, and learning music theory – you will be limited, more so or less, in certain ways. I was a mediocre musician, with moments of inspired playing, now and then, in spite of my limitations. For although I lacked much, I had Heart.

> I'm not a smart man,
> But I know what love is.
> -Forrest Gump

Throughout my career I encountered every manner of musician. There seemed to be two general classes, with exceptions, of course. On the technical side, there were those with dazzling skills, usually schooled, musically, and there were those like myself, who were self-taught and technically limited. But there was another, far more important and essential aspect; there were those, both trained and self-taught, who played with Heart, and those who didn't. As you'd expect, the most amazing players were those few who embodied both technical prowess and Heart. Every band I was in was a mix of these types; each member appreciated for the unique gifts they brought. But the highest moments in my musical life occurred with players who had Heart, whether they were schooled or self-taught.

Each night I performed, I ached to express The Great Sorrow, The Great Beauty, and the Richness born of both, in an Exquisite Anguish of Creativity, with varying degrees of success. But in 17 years, I only fully fulfilled that Passion one afternoon near the end of my career, in a moment that to this day, I don't understand. I think it's one of

   An Affair of the Heart

those things that, however much the mind might dissect it, cannot truly be comprehended.

It was 1976, and I was playing in a band that I loved more than any I'd ever played in, in the finest venue I'd ever played, to audiences that came not simply to drink and carouse, but quite often to listen. On off-nights when we weren't playing, even though there were parties to go to and other bands to enjoy, I longed, instead, to be playing.

One of the guitarists in that band, named Rich, was a fine technician, and a man of Heart, as well. We had played together in several bands, and got on very well, until suddenly, it seemed, he became upset with me during one of our practice sessions, and stayed that way for weeks thereafter.

I finally learned the source of his frustration in a strained conversation one day. He was irritated with me because however good a player I'd become on my own, he felt I could be exceptional if I only realized my full potential through formal study of musical theory and disciplined practice of proper techniques. As it turns out, he was frustrated because he cared. But even after our talk, the situation remained somewhat tense.

In the midst of this situation, the Fulfillment of my musical life came one afternoon as we were practicing in the empty nightclub, on a sweltering Tucson afternoon, with Rich still frustrated with me, and the tension palpable.

My favorite song at that time was written by one of the band members who, like me, had more Heart than skill – not that we were shoddy players, mind you; we'd both become quite good, in

Into the World

our way. The chords of this particular song were, for me, a beautiful canvas on which to pour out one's Heart. And as we practiced that song... well, I can't adequately express what happened, because as I said, I don't really understand, myself.

As the song progressed, I found myself pouring my Whole Being into a musical expression of the Heart that I had carried since childhood, a Feeling that had only deepened through the years; that impossible, heart-rending Union of The Great Sorrow and The Great Joy of life. All sense of myself, the player, vanished, and the Heartbreaking Beauty at the core of my Being bypassed the mind and flowed straight to my fingers on the keyboard. Over so many years of improvisation, I had reached the point where the mind's involvement had long since been minimized; but nothing like this absolute bypassing had occurred. But it wasn't simply the bypassing of the mind; it was the notes that were played, the phrasings, and the tonalities; the totality of their expression.

As I played, tears filled my eyes. And when it came time for my solo, which was always improvised in the moment, the distilled Essence of my Overflowing Heart was, for the first and last time in my musical life, Expressed in its Absolute Fullness, in every note.

In the silence at the end of the song, I simply sat there, embarrassed to turn around, for fear my friends would see my tears. I felt something touch my arm, lightly, and turning just slightly, saw that it was Rich standing there, so close behind me... with tears in his eyes. He had been there during the solo, watching, having walked across the stage during the Outpouring. His mind may have been frustrated by my fingering technique, but the outpouring of my Heart had ignited an outpouring in his.

   An Affair of the Heart

For good or ill, my spiritual life has been much as my musical life. I have never been formally trained in a specific tradition, and I confess that as was the case with music, there are certain deficits born of that. And I've never been given to spiritual practice, not simply because I'm lazy, which I am, but because it seemed too cold, mechanistic and goal-based; too conditional.

What I had Longed for and sought from my earliest youth was not the product of conditionality; not a created state born of doing this or refraining from that. Such notions were anathema to me. What I sought – and I only realized this in my later years – was the Experience of Unconditional Love that did not come and go; a Fullness, Completion, and Bliss that was inherent in the nature of my Being, my Essence, arising from and relying upon nothing, except, perhaps, the simple fact that I exist, that I Am.

Only a few years later, my life as a musician would end. As difficult and fraught with insecurity as that time had been, I would not trade it if I could.

On Having Become Someone

How am I doing?
How do I look?

The Contraction of Individuated Selfhood

I apologize in advance for not being able to adequately describe what I mean by the felt sense of personhood. It's so incredibly complex.

It isn't the sense of individuation that's inherent in our embodied existence; the experience of life and the world through our unique vehicle of perception. Nor is it merely a thought that we hold of our self. These things, and more, are factors, to be sure. But far more essentially, it's the *feeling* within us of our personal self, and how we *feel* about that self. It's our sense of self-esteem, based on the presence or absence of qualities and attributes deemed desirable or not, and the belief that comes about, over time, that those qualities and attributes define who we are, what we are, are aspects of our self.

This felt sense of our personal self is based on a relentless, ongoing self-assessment, and self-judgment born of that assessment. "How

 An Affair of the Heart

am I doing? Am I liked by those I know, and those I meet along the way? Am I admired and respected by those in my field of endeavor? Am I attractive and desirable to those I desire to see me so? And most tragically, am I worthy of love?" And on, and on. This ongoing assessment and judgment becomes a self-generating, self-perpetuating "mechanism" within us.

Primarily it's how others perceive us that comes to define how we perceive ourself, and more importantly, feel about ourself. The relentless concern over stature creates a condition of contraction across the whole of our manifest being – the subtle-energetic, psychological, somatic, and no doubt other aspects of which I'm unaware. It is a feeling, palpable and visceral, that becomes, through identification with it, to be the feeling of "me". And this feeling about ourself, of ourself… that's what I mean by the felt sense of personhood.

For most, the feeling of selfhood is in constant flux, resulting in continuous tension, anxiety, unease, and quite often dissatisfaction. I suspect this *may* be what the Buddha meant by the term "dukkha"; inherent unease and dissatisfaction giving rise to a relentless grasping after things and circumstances, in a desperate effort to divert attention from this inner suffering.

My Experience

I had discovered early on in my Christian youth that I was not like the archetype I held of Jesus, an embodiment of Pure, Selfless Love, with the singular agenda of Healing and Blessing all of creation. I had wanted with all my heart to be that Perfect Being, but quickly discovered I was not, and that more often than not, none of my

On Having Become Someone

heartfelt efforts to become so could stand against the powerful desires and fears that most always motivated me. I came to see that there were, within me, conflicting energies and agendas that could be broken down, perhaps far too simplistically, as selfish and selfless. Of course none of us are purely one or the other, but live somewhere in the middle, only rarely moving in the extremes. But at that time my simple-minded, religiously-born self-criticality tended to see only the extremes, and to judge myself harshly, as having more negative than positive attributes.

During the years of early youth when I was constantly relocating and was the observer, not the participant in human society, this self-criticality had not yet formed. I had come to feel a subtle sense that I was somehow not prone to the lesser aspects of human nature I saw playing out in school after school. But that aloof exceptionalism was only possible because I had not yet moved into society and seen reflected within myself those very qualities and attributes I judged so harshly in others. It was only after I consciously entered society in high school that my studied gaze turned inward upon myself, and I discovered those "lesser" aspects of human nature alive within me; qualities common to all of us embodied here in space and time.

Engaged at last in society, I found myself bound up, more and more deeply, in a relentless concern for stature in every aspect of human experience. For entering more concretely into personhood, the esteem in which I was held by others determined the esteem in which I held my self.

And often, regardless of what others thought of me, the esteem in which I held myself was not always favorable, for I also assessed myself based on my own moralistic inner criteria, independent of external factors. Any lingering sense of aloof exceptionalism was

 An Affair of the Heart

soon destroyed, replaced by increasingly harsh self-judgement.

Of course I knew that like all of us, I was not wholly condemnable, but an ever-modulating play of polarities; sometimes predominantly selfless, other times not, and most often a confounding confluence of the two. I could see within myself the motivations of selfishness, grounded in desire and fear. And through that understanding within myself, found myself able to forgive such motivations in others, feeling compassion for the suffering I knew the situation created in them. But for some reason I was unable to forgive these aspects of my own human nature.

In Hinduism they speak of samskaras and vasanas. Samskaras, according to my limited understanding, are deeply ingrained conditionings, born of varied causes[17]. They are like callouses, bruises, or open wounds in the depths of our Being. These, in turn, give rise to vasanas; tendencies, thoughts, and actions. It appeared that the samskaras and vasanas of moralistic self-judgment that I so despised as an aspect of Christianity in my youth had become, insidiously, more deep-seated within me than I had thought.

Later in life, I came to understand the importance of self-forgiveness as an essential aspect of a mature, balanced, and peaceful life. But at this point that piece of wisdom, and many others, hadn't yet taken root in me. Or, if they had, they lacked the strength to stand against powerful samskaras of self-judgment and condemnation. The nature of my manifest being at that time was having none of redemption and self-forgiveness. The sense of myself, of what I was, having wandered far from the Beatific Ocean of my origin, my Essence, had hardened into a salt doll in the Desert of Personhood,

---

[17] I beg the forgiveness of Hindu scholars.

On Having Become Someone

and failing to see and forgive the complexity of its own nature, held itself in ever-increasing contempt and disdain.

> I reveled in the praise of my teachers,
> And saw how, in receiving good grades,
> Mom and Dad were made happy and proud.
>
> And so, I sought academic stature,
> That I might gain praise, or so I thought,
> But truly, it was only Love I sought…
>
> Causeless, and Unconditional.
>
> I saw how the girl I found beautiful,
> Was drawn to certain qualities,
> And features of a certain kind.
>
> And so, I sought romantic stature,
> That I might be adored, or so I thought,
> But truly, it was only Love I sought…
>
> Causeless, and Unconditional.
>
> I saw how those in my profession,
> Admired and respected those peers,
> With knowledge, skill, and experience.
>
> And so, I sought professional stature,
> That I might gain respect, or so I thought,
> But truly, it was only Love I sought…
>
> Causeless, and Unconditional.

An Affair of the Heart

In every aspect of life I came to rely,
On the estimation, by others, of myself,
For my own sense of "worth".

Worth as one praised,
Worth as one desirable,
Worth as one respected…

Worth as one…Lovable.

Somewhere along the way, I lost,
The Fullness, Completion, and Bliss,
Inherent in my Essence…

Shining simply because I Am.

Somewhere along the way, I lost,
The Experience at the Heart of Being,
Of Love Shining, without condition…

Simply because I Am.

What irony that the pain of bondage,
To the intercessor self, bound to stature,
Would be the very fire that drove me…
Within, to my Essence, long forgotten.

Where, Held in The Beloved's Embrace,
Conditionality consumed by the Fire of Grace,
I Swooned in the Ecstasy of Being…

Simply because I Am.

A Preface on Teachers

'Tis the Wine, not the bottle,
that Intoxicates.

I feel it's necessary to add, at this point, a preface to the chapters that follow, in which I'll be describing experiences had while in relationship with various spiritual teachers. In this book I will not mention the names of any teachers. It's not that I'm ungrateful or intend disrespect. Rather, I don't want any controversies or judgments surrounding the teachers to distract from your consideration of my experiences, which are difficult enough to accept without veiling them in such controversies or judgments.

> For the Teacher, one has gratitude,
> But love and devotion is for God.
> -Hazrat Inayat Khan

One of the most dangerous tendencies I've observed in both teachers and students is for more to be made of a teacher's station than

 An Affair of the Heart

should be made[18]. So often, it seems, teachers plant a flag at a particular station[19], and declare the summit attained. They declare themselves "fully" enlightened, a "master", or even more exalted, an avatar[20].

Another dangerous tendency is for students – in some traditions more than others, it seems – to make more than should be made of the person of the teacher, the vehicle through which spiritual power might be manifested. In some religious traditions this tendency is actually institutionalized, opening up the possibility of corruption at the hands of teachers in whom egoity, the "lesser" self, is still substantially present.

Every so-called "enlightened" teacher with whom I've been in relationship has proven to be simply a human being who had arrived at a certain station, was spiritually gifted in various ways, but was by no means perfected in all aspects of being. In short, I have not found the Christ-like archetype I had naively hoped, early on, to discover; utterly selfless, refined and perfected in all aspects of being, full and complete within, free of lack, living only to Heal and Bless out of Boundless Compassion and Causeless, Conditionless Love.

The list is long of "enlightened" teachers who have been profoundly eloquent of speech, beautiful of countenance, imbued with spiritual power, or otherwise gifted, who went on to display human frailties ranging from that woundedness which is common to us all, to

---

[18] A spiritual friend once declared, as we drove home from seeing my third teacher, "Oh, these 'enlightened' ones, always making more of themselves than should be made." I found this to be a brilliantly succinct assessment, and have used the phrase "more than should be made" ever since.

[19] Sufism speaks of states and stations; states being divine gifts of some kind, whether transient or enduring, and stations being states of being that we become established in along The Way.

[20] An incarnation of God.

A Preface on Teachers

pathological brokenness. For me, at 72 years of age, after a lifetime of engaging with or observing teachers from a distance, it's come to this:

> The Greatness of a teacher is not in their spiritual power,
> Their beauty, eloquence, intelligence, charisma,
> Or the number of their followers.
>
> The Greatness of a teacher, or anyone for that matter,
> Is the extent to which the lesser self,
> Has been subsumed by Love.

Much has been written these days about the continued functioning of samskaras[21] and vasanas after enlightenment or awakening, and the need for continued attention to, and refinement of different aspects of our Being. I refer you to those writings for more in-depth discussion. Although I suspect anyone reading this book may be familiar with these things, perhaps through first-hand experience.

Cautionary notes aside, I received invaluable teachings from my teachers, however much their lesser selves had yet to be subsumed by Love.

With my first teacher I was shown, in my own direct experience, that there is more to life than meets the eye. The Mystical nature of existence that I'd formerly dismissed as mythology or the delusional imaginings of hysterical religionists was, in fact, real. Not necessarily real in the ways that the various traditions interpreted and presented, or in the ways that the teacher himself presented,

---

[21] In Hinduism, samskaras are deeply ingrained conditionings, born of varied causes. They are like callouses, bruises, or open wounds in the depths of our Being. These, in turn, give rise to vasanas; tendencies, thoughts, and actions arising as a result of samskaras.

An Affair of the Heart

but real in my own direct experience, unwrapped in any particular interpretation or ideology.

In relationship with all of my teachers, I was shown that my naive notions about enlightenment and the enlightened were simply that; naive. In particular was my experience of the emanation of spiritual energy and the phenomena associated with it. My assumption that such emanation and phenomena indicated a perfected being was quickly corrected.

In spending time with teachers of different spiritual traditions, I learned that I needn't accept the theologies or descriptions of "reality" that they or anyone else purported as "truth". Each of my teachers interpreted their states and stations from their own perspectives, based on a variety of factors. Other teachers taught different views and stances regarding what appeared to be the same or similar states and stations. The more I learned about the history and scope of religion and spirituality, the more I saw the broad spectrum of interpretations held forth as "Truth", and the many theories and theologies held forth as "reality". I saw my own transient experiences and stations described in these various faiths, but interpreted, always, in ways unique to each.

Friends mock me lovingly, to this day, for my continuing desire to find a teacher; one who needn't be perfected in all aspects of being, but whose person has been more deeply subsumed by Love than my own; this subsuming, this Love being the single most important flame to which I am drawn these days.

The spiritual path in which the Mystical Emanation of spiritual energy transmutes the Hearts of friends, has been bitterly tarnished in the decades since Eastern Mysticism arrived in the West. Teacher after

A Preface on Teachers

teacher, supposedly free of bondage to the lesser aspects of human nature, has proven to be otherwise. But however disheartening that may be, it did not, for me, negate the reality of my direct experience. It only indicated that those in whom the "person" has been transmuted and subsumed by The Inner Radiance are rare.

As Rumi is purported to have said:

> "It is not astonishing or strange that a holy person, whose nature has been transformed, who has been delivered from individuality, transformed by God's Light, can transmute into gold the copper of another's existence, can illumine another and make him reach the Ocean of Illumination of 'All things return to God'. There is nothing astonishing or strange about this!"

 # An Affair of the Heart

The First Teacher of Significance

What Was That?!

The Great Suffering

Over the years The Great Sorrow, Existential Fear, and the felt sense of myself as a person merged into what I came to call The Great suffering; a Spiritual Suffering in my deepest interiority that impacted every aspect of my manifest being and ongoing experience. It might seem that such a state would stamp out the ember of spiritual aspiration, but in fact, it was the primary driver of the desire to be free, primarily of the pain of personhood as I experienced it. For when we are on fire, our mind has no time for idle considerations. There is only one desire; to be free of fire.

But lest I paint too bleak a picture, of course I did not spend every moment wallowing in despair, awash in The Great Suffering. Except in moments of deepest despair The Great Suffering remained as a background ambience in moment-to-moment experience, sometimes closer, sometimes far distant. But make no mistake, this ambient pain aside, I Reveled in the joys of embodied existence. I delighted in – to paraphrase the common saying – wine, romance, and song. I was not debauched, but neither was I saintly. But always,

 An Affair of the Heart

in both my "higher" moments and my "lower", The Great Suffering was present to some degree. And as the years passed, it become ever more present and painful in the forefront of experience.

The presence of The Great Suffering may seem a great misfortune, but some of us need a fire on the savannah to drive the lion of Attention[22] within.

> For some, it takes a fire on the savannah,
> To drive the lion of Attention within,
> Returning in fearful flight...
>
> To shelter, in the Cave of the Heart.
> For some, without those Flames,
> Attention wanders creation endlessly,
> Moving in outward fascination.
>
> There are those requiring no such fire,
> But such was not my nature,
> Driven, as I was, by a Great Suffering.
>
> Fleeing that most Ancient of Pains,
> I was driven to that Place, within,
> Where I rested without Fear...
>
> And drank from Living Waters.

---

[22] The focal point of Awareness.

The First Teacher of Significance

I thank that Fiery, Painful Blessing,
That chased me like a Fierce Friend,
Until, at last, it saw me safely Embraced…
In The Arms of The Beloved.

The Letter

In 1980, on my 30th birthday, I sat alone in my room, overcome by The Great Suffering, which had finally overwhelmed my desperate attempts to fend it off through distraction, or flee it through other diversions. I began writing, to God, to whatever invisible force could help, even though I had no faith whatsoever. Such was the state of my desperation.

The lines of most import in that letter would turn out to be, "The healthy have no need of a physician. Help." Tearful throughout the writing, I was finally overcome. I got up from my chair, and as I started walking away, fell to the floor, sobbing.

It appears that my heartfelt prayer was heard, for the very next day my girlfriend gave me a spiritual book for my birthday that impacted me deeply, and was a great comfort. I delved into other spiritual books, and in one way or another they gave comfort for the year and a half it would take before an event occurred that would change my life unalterably, far more than words on a page could ever hope to do.

Our First Meeting

By 1981 it had become clear that my career as a musician was coming to an end, and an existential crisis loomed large in my ongoing experience. In the midst of this psychological and spiritual

An Affair of the Heart

crisis, I began re-reading *Autobiography of a Yogi*, wanting desperately to believe that the Mystical reality it portrayed might be true, for the reality of life as I'd come to experience it had become unbearable. Reading the autobiography was a strained affair, for as much as spiritual books had comforted me on a certain level, I had long ago abandoned belief in the Mystical, the unprovable, and had come to hold faith with a lip-curling disdain. I had become quite bitter and cynical.

Cynicism aside, in the Autobiography I found myself enamored of the chapter about Master Mahasaya, a disciple of the Indian saint, Ramakrishna, and a devotee, as well, of The Divine Mother. This "imagined" Divine Mother had, in my desperation, become the object of my prayers. I had no faith in such a Being, and felt foolish talking to Her, pleading with Her for Mercy, for Help. But as had been the case since my early youth, the deep Longing for Unconditional Love was simply a part of my nature, and so I prayed to an imaginary Being that for me embodied that quality. As the saying goes, "There are as many paths to God as souls on earth." It seems I've always been inherently devotional – in both its greater and lesser aspects – even while fiercely empirical; qualities at perpetual war with one another.

In November of '81 a spiritual friend called to tell me she'd seen a spiritual teacher who was, in her estimation, enlightened, and recommended I go see him. He was giving a series of talks and meditations for a month or so on different evenings each week. Trust of my friend's intuition and intelligence weighed heavily against my cynicism. I'd never actually seen a so-called enlightened spiritual teacher, and cynicism aside, curiosity got the better of me.

The next meditation was that Monday evening, the 9th of November.

The First Teacher of Significance

I was still playing music for a living and had to start playing at 9 o'clock. I felt a little anxiety around the fact that if I went to the meditation, I'd have to find a way to slip out of the hall after only a brief stay, without seeming rude.

I arrived and was stunned to see so many people there. I had no idea spirituality was such a "thing" in San Diego, which seemed such a conservative community. As it turned out, my anxiety about leaving early was put to rest, because the teacher suggested that instead of a longer meditation, we do a series of brief meditations. I'd taken a seat near the exit, and his plan would allow me a chance to slip away, unnoticed, after the first meditation.

I had no idea how to meditate. In spite of having read some of the classic spiritual books from the 60s and 70s, and considering myself, in spite of all my cynicism, to be a "spiritual" guy, I had never sat to meditate. Somehow it had always seemed anathema to me, for reasons too complex to explain here, without derailing this story. Thankfully, the teacher said not to do any techniques we might have learned. We were to keep our eyes open, and keep a "loose gaze" upon him. That seemed crazy to me, and highly suspicious. When he started playing a CD of music before the meditation began, I became even more incredulous.

I sat there, just relaxing, gazing as he'd said, listening to the music, which I actually found fascinating. And then, to my utter amazement, I noticed that my entire field of vision began to change. I saw a strange white light overlaying everything, intensifying quickly. The heads of those in front of me became as if molten gold, a brilliant translucence that to this day, I've never been able to adequately describe. I blinked again and again, and the light remained. If one of the people in front of me moved their head, the space their head

 An Affair of the Heart

formerly occupied was black, like a film negative, and the gold light followed them as they moved. In time, the light absorbed everything and everyone, and all I could see was the teacher, surrounded by that light, but sharply, clearly visible, while everything else had dissolved in a field of the most Beautiful Luminosity.

It wasn't only a visual astonishment. My state of Being changed. I couldn't explain then, and can't now. It wasn't a peace that washed over me, or stillness, or silence, or any of what I'd read might occur in meditation. It was more like an Aliveness, as if my own Aliveness had been lit up from the inside out. A dying Ember in my Heart was being blown upon, so to speak, and had brightened. I sat through the meditation simply dumbfounded.

The meditation ended, and thankfully, I was able to slip out unnoticed, and head to the trashy bar where I was currently playing. I had no idea what had happened, but was inspired by the possibility that perhaps, just perhaps, there was truly something to all of the spirituality I'd read about for so many years, but had come to dismiss as hallucination, delusion, and religious hysteria.

I Go Up

I woke up the next day and my Experience of Being – what it felt like to be alive – was dramatically altered; unlike anything I'd ever experienced. I could not, for the first time in memory, feel The Great Sorrow, or Existential Fear, or the terrible contraction of personhood. All of these, The Great Suffering, had Vanished from Awareness.

All perceptions and sensations were simply appearing in a Field of Awareness, as I came to call it, that "I" now was. But it was an "I" that was not individuated, separate; not the person I'd become over

The First Teacher of Significance

a lifetime. There was no intercessor self, veiling all of experience.

> I did not feel myself expanded as all that is,
> A part of everything, and everything a part of me.
>
> Nor did I feel myself as "That" within which all appears,
> The Absolute, everything arising within me.
>
> I did not feel "myself" at all.
>
> Unless, by "I" you mean…
> This… All of This, Aliveness, Now.
>
> Not a thing alive,
> But… Aliveness Itself.
>
> There was no place,
> Where "This" ended, and I began.

I did feel the Vehicle of Perception in a "notional" sense, of course. For there was seeing through these eyes, touching with these hands, feeling these feet on the earth. There was movement through space and time; the body was here, and the chair was there.

The only difference was – a difference too astounding to describe adequately – I could not feel the felt sense of myself, that contraction, density, and objectification that had been felt both psychologically and, perhaps more importantly, somatically.

I wanted to run down the street shouting, "Oh my God, it's real! It's real! It's true! The impossible-to-believe things that you've read… they're not delusion or religious hysteria!"

 An Affair of the Heart

This was not a Blissful state, imbued with the Ecstasy of Being. Rather, it was a state of Serene Emptiness; empty of all Inner Suffering, empty of the felt sense of myself as the object-perceiver-experiencer-person. It was an experience that I would later come to call Liberation; a lofty sounding word, but one worthy of use here. For Awareness was Liberated from the terrible contraction of individuation and self-identity.

Three days passed in this incredible state. And then…

I Come Down

When I awoke on the fourth day, I felt it… the first subtle inklings of the old state of Being; not just the felt sense of myself, but the Gordian Knot of contraction across the whole of my Being; Spiritual Unhappiness. It was subtle at first, but unmistakable, and terrible. It rolled in slowly over that day and the next, like a tide reclaiming its lost beachhead.

Although The Great Suffering seemed to creep gradually back into Awareness, its appearance was actually a binary experience, for with the first microbial speck of its reappearance, an end was put to the Absoluteness of what had been.

The return of The Great Suffering was so horrifying to me, so unbearably painful – especially given its juxtaposition to the experience of Liberation – that I became nearly bedridden for several days. What had happened? Why had the wonderful experience vanished? The mind raced to discover a cause, moving in concepts of conditionality. Was it something I had done; something I hadn't done? But seeking such conditional causes, of course, only poured

The First Teacher of Significance

gasoline on the fire. Such seeking was indicative of individuation and personhood, inherent in the very nature of that condition.

After several days of lying in bed and pacing the apartment in despair, I thought I would try to recapture the experience by meditating on my own. After all, the experience seemed to have been caused by meditating with the teacher. So I went into the small bedroom closet and shut the door behind me.

Sitting there, turning Attention within, I felt nothing of that Serene Emptiness within; only the prattling, frenetic mind and the felt sense of contraction and unease. I saw that the contraction was both of mind and body. If the notions of a subtle body I had read about were true, I felt that it, too, was squirming in discomfort, writhing to free itself, but to no avail. The only subtle perception was of a hollowness inside, in the shape of a tornado, widening as it approached my head.

I gave up my failed attempt at meditating and called the friend who had recommended I see the teacher. Perhaps I was doing something wrong? Perhaps I simply didn't know how to meditate? Since she was far more experienced in such matters, I asked her for every meditation technique she knew of.

In desperation, a week or so after having seen the teacher, after going up, and coming down, then flailing for a time in despair, I drove up the coast to the beautiful gardens of the Self Realization

An Affair of the Heart

Fellowship[23] (SRF) in Encinitas to try once again to meditate using the techniques described by my friend; to somehow recapture what had been, and then was not, something known, then forgotten.

---

[23] The spiritual organization founded by Paramahansa Yogananda.

The Journey to The Kingdom of Heaven

What if you knew little of the walled villages,
Of religion, belief, faith, and philosophy,
And then experienced, one day,
What seemed, when considered after the fact,
A loss of consciousness,
The vanishing of Everything from Awareness,
Including yourself as the one aware, and yet…

Awareness continued.

And what if the nature of that Awareness,
Pure and unsullied by space, time, and objects,
In which even you, the experiencer, had vanished,
Was so Ineffably Sublime that words did not exist,
To express its Ecstasy, its Rapture, its Perfection,
The Fulfillment of your Heart's Desire,
An Experience worthy of the phrase…

The Kingdom of Heaven, within.

An Affair of the Heart

It was Sunday, November 15th, 1981, if memory serves me rightly, that I drove north to the Self Realization Fellowship gardens, and found a place that, sadly, was only somewhat secluded; a nook by the old pool, long emptied due to its sitting on top of a deteriorating cliff that had already claimed a Kali temple built nearby. I wasn't a member of SRF, but these exquisite gardens are, thankfully, open to the public. The clifftop gardens overlook the Pacific, and from my bench I could see the vast expanse, and hear the waves breaking far below.

After sitting awhile, unconscious of who might see me, I began sobbing, unable to stand against an inner tsunami of The Great Suffering, which had returned with a vengeance after the previous weeks experience. Its inherent despair had swept into forgetfulness all that was Beautiful in life, and all that was Joyful within. I found myself gasping, psychically drowning in The Great Sorrow, weary and exhausted by Existential Fear, and unable to bear the pain inherent in personhood[24].

Cursing the Gods

At some point my tearful Sorrow gave way to the unbridled Rage that was an aspect of The Great Sorrow. Rage at the notions of God I'd read of, and the heartbreaking conditionality of that God's Love I found in the theologies I'd come across. Rage at the confounding notions of enlightenment, and the fact that according to scripture,

---
[24] See the chapter On Having Become Someone.

The Journey to The Kingdom of Heaven

although multitudes hear of it, few set about the Journey, and only a handful attain. For I was neither a saint nor a disciplined practitioner. Was there no end to this terrible pain for those like myself? Was there no Unconditional, Causeless Love for those like myself? Was it all based on the accrual of merit, in whatever form the varied scriptures declared it to be?

I surrendered completely to that rage, which I had held back all of my life, no longer caring for the supposed consequences I'd read of. Let a vengeful God curse me for my blasphemy. I would expect no less from such a Demonic Judge. For the "Divine Plan" seemed to me not something born in Heaven by a Merciful God, but devised in the bowels of hell by the fallen angel himself. Who else would conceive such a heartless scheme of reward and punishment, of Love bound in cruel conditionality. What contemptuous father would require the torturous death of his son as recompense for the imperfections of inherently imperfect Beings? If that was Divine Love, I stood against it for all eternity. It mattered not that I was an insignificant microbe in the infinite creation; this insignificant microbe declared itself an enemy of such a God. However futile, like the fate of Sisyphus, I would stand for all eternity against this Architect of Hell, this Father of Sorrows. God, as I'd come to understand such a Being to be, should have been put in chains and tried for crimes against creation.

One by one, from Jesus to Buddha, I called before me every teacher, every god or goddess I had read of, and tears still streaming, cursed them with unrestrained ferocity, with unbridled Rage.

 An Affair of the Heart

How Can You Be So Cruel?

Last in the list of gods and goddesses that came to mind for my Wrath was Divine Mother. I had only recently re-read the story of Master Mahasaya in Yogananda's autobiography, and recalled how the Divine Mother with whom Master Mahasaya was in relationship was all that I had always dreamed God should be; the embodiment of Unconditional Love, Compassion, and Mercy. But such a being seemed to me now, more than ever in my life, a mere fairytale, an unforgivable lie propagated on the foolish and naive, the desperately imagined but illusory hope of the hopeless. For in my life, in spite of so many tearful cries over so many decades, I'd seen no evidence of such a Being, much less come to any direct experience.

All of that said, when I imagined Her before me, my tears increased almost in an instant, and Absolute Rage turned to Absolute Sorrow. Instead of cursing Her, I sobbed from the deepest depths of my Soul, "How could You be so cruel?!"

Blinded by tears, I closed my eyes, and abandoning all hope, indeed abandoning my life, sat there, drowning in pain, breathing The Great Suffering in and out. I could no longer discern the aggregate aspects of this Suffering; it had long since become a singular Agony, its spices having dissolved indistinguishably into the Masala of its totality.

The Journey to The Kingdom of Heaven

A note on what is to follow:

Many of the insights or revelations that I describe in what follows seem like obvious facts that anyone with a modicum of discernment should know. But it was the uncommon intensity, the breadth and depth of their impact across my Being, not confined merely to intellectual understanding, that made them, in the moments described, Angels guiding my way to the Fulfillment of my Heart's Desire. We can hear something again and again, to no avail, then suddenly, one day, be impacted. A seemingly insipid platitude heard endlessly over time, causing our lip to curl in disdain, in the right moment cracks open our Heart.

It's also important to note that I had no knowledge at this time of Hinduism's Advaita (nondual) vedantic philosophy, or of that tradition's method of Self Enquiry. What ensued was simply me reasoning with myself, moved forward, step by step, by the empirical evidence that presented itself, experientially.

I Cannot Stop My Heart

I felt that I could not bear existing one moment longer. Eyes still closed, sinking ever more deeply into The Great Suffering, I thought to consciously stop my heart. And with all the intensity I could muster, I gave it my all. But my heart didn't stop beating.

Even though any sensible person knows you can't will your heart to stop, and even though I knew this, myself, in this moment the failure came as a shock to me. For although I'd never really considered the matter deeply (who would), I evidently held to an assumption

 An Affair of the Heart

that my volition, my engagement was somehow involved in, and requisite to the functioning of the body. After all, it was "my" body, and an integral part of what I considered "me". And yet, my heart did not obey my willful command. I went on to try and stop my breath, but found that my lungs, too, were having none of my imperious dictates.

An Aside:

For students of nondual philosophy this revelation may seem elementary and obvious, as the notion, "You are not the body-mind" is a foundational principle. But having never studied that philosophy, the revelations that came to me were utterly fresh and new, and shocking in a way that can only happen when that is the case. I was not, in this process, remembering a process I had read of or experiencing anything already "known" intellectually; my enquiry was unguided by the known, and my Knowing was experiential.

One Sensation Among Many

Having focused so intensely on the heart and lungs, I became aware of other sensations within the body, and realized what had never been obvious to me before; that The Great Suffering was actually felt in the body, locatable among the other bodily sensations, not simply an amorphous, unlocatable psycho-emotional feeling. Its locus seemed to be in the solar plexus, below the heart, above the navel. But its radius was indistinct, its boundary dissolved indistinguishably into the masala of ongoing experience. It had long

The Journey to The Kingdom of Heaven

since become an aspect of simply what it felt like to be alive.

And it occurred to me that in the same instant I felt the sensation of The Great Suffering, I also heard a bird singing in a nearby tree, the sound of waves breaking below the cliffs; I felt the warmth of the sun on my face, a cooling ocean breeze, the pressure of my body against the stone bench upon which I sat, and myriad other inner sensations, as well.

The Great Suffering was, I realized, merely one of many perceptions and sensations appearing to me, both outer and inner, in any given moment. And in the instant of realizing that, I became aware of all of the sensations and perceptions arising to me… all at once.

The Field of Awareness

Previously, in moments of contracted awareness when I focused acutely on something or other, the object of focus, whether objective or internal, pleasant or unpleasant, had given rise to specific psychological and somatic responses. But in this ambient awareness of everything-all at-once there were no such responses. A subtle relaxation spread through me, and I experienced, as I had several days before, the felt sense of myself as a formless Field of Awareness. I "Remembered" that experience of a few days prior not through conventional memory, but with the Whole of my Being.

And a whispered question arose within me; a shocking question, even in its subtlety and simplicity; "What am I? What *is* this Field of Awareness that feels like "me", like what I am?" Later in life I would learn of the advaitic question, "Who am I?" made famous by the Hindu saint, Ramana Maharshi. But I knew "who" I was.

 An Affair of the Heart

That question, to me, had to do with the person. Rather, I was questioning "what". What was I before the "who" came to be? What was I, Essentially.

Everything Wrapped in the Known

Eyes still closed, it struck me, again with uncommon intensity, that the sensations and perceptions that appeared to me, whether internal or external, were all wrapped in "meaning". In the very instant I heard the sound of birdsong in a distant tree, the word "bird" came to mind, along with an inner image, and all of the knowledge and subsequent feelings I had acquired over time regarding that sound and the creature that made it.

Hearing the sound of the bird, up, to my left, in a nearby tree, I realized that even my relationship to spatiality – to up, down, front, back, left, and right – was overlaid with acquired knowledge and accompanying psychological and somatic conditionings and responses. Though very subtle, these became apparent to me.

Likewise, within the darkness behind my closed eyes I saw a world of colors and gradations of light; colors that had names and psycho-emotional connotations, each invoking a unique response; responses made obvious to me in that moment, in spite of their previously unperceived subtlety.

These recognitions were not simply of the mind. For as had been the case in my earlier experience, several days before, I felt a separation of "myself", the perceiver-experiencer, from all that was perceived and experienced.

The Journey to The Kingdom of Heaven

It dawned on me that over the course of my life the Immediacy of experience had become veiled, overlaid with the already known; an overlaying that had become an unconscious, reflexive condition. This overlaying applied not just to all that the senses provided, within and without, but to the totality of experience itself; simply what it felt like to be alive.

And the question arose, "Is it possible to experience existence free of the veiling overlays of the known?"

The Known, Acquired

And in one of the most important insights of this enquiry – a simple and obvious thing, but in the context of that moment, crucially pivotal – it dawned on me that this overlaying of experience with the known had *not* always been the case. And more specifically relevant to the moment, the aggregates of The Great Suffering – Horror, Sorrow, Rage, Existential Fear, and the Unbearable Contraction of Self-Identity – had not always been present in my awareness.

Horror, and sorrow at the suffering of the world had come about as I learned of the darker aspects of Nature and humankind. Existential Fear had arisen as I encountered the tenuous nature of sustaining my existence. And most essential to my enquiry, the felt sense of my personal self, all that I had come to take myself to be, had also been acquired over time.

At this revelation there was a certain Liberation on the level of mind, but energetically and somatically, the contraction remained.

   An Affair of the Heart

All of the aspects of The Great Suffering were not innate elements of my Awareness, were not *native* to "me", or my Experience of Existing. There had been a time in my infancy and very early youth when I had not yet learned language or gained any "knowledge" of the world or myself; a time when nothing had yet accrued upon the Purity of my Naked Essence.

> There was a time when my Soul was yet unclothed,
> By all that would accrue upon my Naked Innocence,
> When the Ecstasy of Being was unveiled by selfhood,
> And I existed as my Essence.
>
> There was a time, before I learned a language,
> Before the inner voice began its endless chatter,
> Before I came to feel myself the thinker,
> When I was simply Perception.
>
> There was a time before all that is experienced,
> Was wrapped in words, concepts, and images,
> Overlaying every perception with the already known,
> And I was simply Immediacy.
>
> There was a time, before the felt sense of myself,
> Qualified and conditioned in countless ways,
> Came to feel dense, isolated, and alone,
> A time when I was simply Experience.
>
> There was a time, before boy-girl; fat-thin, gifted-dim;
> Smart-dull; attractive-ugly; admired-disdained,
> A time before qualifications and attributions,
> When I simply Was.

The Journey to The Kingdom of Heaven

Might it be Possible?

And the question arose, "Might it be possible to come to the Experience of Being I had known before the constituents of The Great Suffering clouded the Sky of my Essence?" For that Essence was, after all, "me", the real me, the Essential me. Could not the Veils of Suffering, like clothing, be removed, and the Naked Essence revealed?

In the quest I was about to undertake, Mind and Heart, Discernment-Understanding and Feeling-Experience journeyed together, each playing a role in their respective time, according to their respective efficacies. The mind would continue, for a time, to lead the way, bringing me, through discernment and discrimination, to a profoundly shockingly and impactful clarity and recognition of all that had accrued, all that was not my Essence. But as the mind reached the end of its utility, Feeling[25], and the Heart, would take me to the Experience of "what I Am".

> The mind will lead you to Heaven's Gate,
> But there, in Humility, will stop and say,
>
> I have given you all I can,
> And have brought you as far as I am able.
>
> At this juncture, I have become blind.
> At this juncture, I have become mute.
>
> I have shown you what you are not,
> Revealing what you mistook yourself to be.

---

[25] In the coming years my teacher of advaita (nonduality) would often refer to Feeling Enquiry, and I feel strongly that the approach I would take in my enquiry, unwittingly, was what he was referring to. But that, of course, is mere supposition.

An Affair of the Heart

Knowing, now, what you are not,
I have left you Wondering,
Here, at the Gate of Heaven,
What is this formless Knower that I Am?

What is this formless Knower,
That you cannot locate as an object, within,
That, being formless, you cannot "describe",
But which, though formless and unlocatable…

You can Feel as the very Essence of Being,
Within which space and time appear,
Within which the world of objects appears,
Within which… the felt sense "I Am" arises.

I cannot enter here,
Into the Inner Sanctum…
Where Knower and known vanish,
In the Experience of Pure Being.

Nor can "you" enter,
As long as you cling to me.
For I will keep "you" alive,
Thinking endlessly "about".

To enter Here, you must fall,
Heartlong into Feeling…
And Experience What You Are,
Before "you" and Creation ever were.

The Journey to The Kingdom of Heaven

Only when you enter and return, Illumined,
Will I be able to join You There.
And together, You and I, Mind and Heart,
Will Dance in Timeless Eternity.

The Union of Lover and Beloved,
In the Embrace of Dissolution…
In which both Vanish, having never been,
Leaving Love Alone, Beyond All Duality.

Now… at this fateful inner juncture,
Bid me farewell, abandoning all thought,
And Rest in the Feeling of your Essence,
The Unlocatable Aliveness you've come to.

Don't float shallowly Here, in mentation,
But Drown ever more Deeply in Feeling…
Until the last ever-so-subtle vestiges,
Of yourself as one who exists, Vanish…

And You Remain, no longer "you",
As the Kingdom of Heaven, within,
In the Fullness, Completion, and Ecstasy,
Of Nonexistent Existence.

Poof!

Feeling Enquiry

And so, on an inner quest to discover my Essential Being, unshrouded by all that had been acquired over the course of my life, all that was not native to me, I began abandoning engagement with the various sensations and perceptions that appeared to Awareness. I did not do this by struggling with them, fighting to push them away. Rather, as I had done briefly during my earlier attempt at meditation, I moved Attention into a one-pointed focus, this time not on a location within the body, or within the Field of Awareness, but upon Awareness itself; upon the unlocatable, ambient *Feeling* of an Inner Radiance of Aliveness that I was now beginning to Feel and recognize as the Feeling of "me", of "I"[26].

I had reached a point where, through discernment and discrimination, I had discovered, irrefutably, that I could not locate myself as an object-perceiver-experiencer, somewhere within. I could not *find* myself, but – and this is perhaps the most crucial aspect of my enquiry – *I could Feel myself.*

Just as I'd come to feel everything that was present in the Field of Awareness, I could now *Feel* the Field Itself; and that Field was undeniably the Feeling of myself. There was an *Aliveness* (vibration is too unrefined a term) in that Empty Sky within which all perception appeared, and that Aliveness was unmistakably "me", the Subject of all experience, now struggling to experience itself alone.

Fierce Intensity

This enquiry required an uncommon intensity of focus, and a reassertion of that focus, again, and again, and again to push through and past the gravitational pull of habituated, reflexive conditionings

---

[26] I cannot stress how important it is that I had moved from intellectual enquiry into Feeling Enquiry; Feeling myself as the Aliveness within. In the coming years I would read of the Indian sage, Ramana Maharshi, describing a method of enquiry in which you find the "I" Feeling, and rest deeply there.

The Journey to The Kingdom of Heaven

that were, themselves, powerful and relentless, drawing Attention, again and again, into engagement with all that appeared in Awareness, and away from Awareness itself, from the "I" Feeling. If the pain of The Great Suffering had not been so overwhelming, and my desire to escape it such a desperate motivation, I would never have been able to garner the intensity of focus that I sustained throughout this quest. I would find myself able to focus on the "I" Feeling for a time, and then suddenly "come to", seeing that without realizing it, I had slipped off into thought "about" what was happening, or otherwise become engaged with something other than the "I" Feeling. And in that slipping off into thought, the felt sense of myself as the thinker was reasserted, again, and again, and again. But again, and again, and again I refocused Attention back, behind, before, into the Feeling of myself, within which thought arose; into the Feeling of myself as the Source from which Attention moved; prior to that movement; prior to the arising of everything other than the Feeling of Aliveness, Awareness, my Essence.

Singularity of Perception and Sensation

In time, relentlessly pulling Attention back, behind, before all that appeared in Awareness, both the outer and inner worlds of differentiated perceptions and sensations eventually vanished into a perceptual singularity. I no longer had any sense of space, time, or my body. All sense of locatability was gone. I was conscious, with only the most subtle sense of myself as a formless experiencer remaining[27].

---

[27] My second teacher of significance, who I met several years after this day at SRF, would sometimes say, "Feel yourself 'behind'." From the experience this day, I was able to understand what he meant. Of course "behind" is, in a certain sense metaphorical. But in another sense, difficult to explain textually, quite accurate.

An Affair of the Heart

The only movement within Awareness was the now diminished movement of thought, which had become an almost entirely pre-verbal cognition.

Thought and Mind

As I had progressed in my enquiry, the inner voice of the thinking mind had come to be seen as an object of perception, no different than any other. For examining it closely, I saw that there was no moment in time, between thoughts, when "I", the supposed thinker, decided what to think next. That river of verbalization simply flowed, much like my breath and heartbeat, whether I chose to be involved, or not. "My" involvement was not the driving force. I was not "the thinker" in the sense I had always taken myself to be. At some point in my life, this language-based self-dialog had simply taken on a life of its own, rolling along in an impulsive, self-generating current and continuum of reactivity. Again, this seems obvious to anyone who's investigated the matter, but for me, in this moment, it became Shockingly Impactful.

Although the stream of verbalized thought continued, it became like a distant sound, barely noticed, for my relentless focus was on the Feeling of myself, within which thought, and all perceptions-sensations arose. And yet, in a way that I cannot adequately describe, even to myself, verbalized thought was now tied somehow to the functioning of what I can only describe as a pre-verbal Mind which, at this point, seemed to originate from me; to be "mine", or a functioning of "me"; an aspect of my manifest-but-formless Essence. This inner verbalization was simply voicing, in English, a pre-verbal movement of "something else" – of interest, curiosity, fascination, concern – that I had never been aware of before.

The Journey to The Kingdom of Heaven

This, I felt, must be ever so close to the state I had known in early childhood, before language – in even the most subtle sense I was then experiencing – and the accrual of the known, before the felt sense of myself as an object-perceiver-experiencer-person had come about. For that contraction of identity had now become so diminished as to be transparent, apparitional[28].

What, then, am I?

Even in this state of ever-more-subtle Mind and ever deepening Dissolution into and as the "I" Feeling, The Great Question remained; "What, then, am I?"; the question distilled, now, to a nearly pre-verbal movement of Mind. For again, what could not be found as an object, could be Felt, unmistakably, as Attention, the focal point of Awareness, was Dissolving, more and more, into its object of fascination; the formless Ocean from which it arose, and had wandered in outer fascination all of my life.

As Attention Dissolved ever more deeply into and as the felt sense of myself, into that formless Aliveness, and all differentiation vanished, increasingly, from Awareness, the Feeling of my Essence began to have, ever so subtly at first, but increasingly so, a Desirability, becoming subtly Enjoyable and "Attractive" to Attention.

Whereas my enquiry had previously been moved by Repulsion – the desire to be rid of The Great Suffering that had filled Awareness (now nowhere to be found) – I was now experiencing the first, ever so subtle inklings of Attraction, of Desire for the Enjoyment of this

---

[28] In Hinduism, this is referred to as savikalpa samadhi, where only the subtlest sense of a subject-perceiver-experiencer remains in Awareness. In nirvikalpa samadhi, this last vestige of subjectivity Vanishes.

An Affair of the Heart

Feeling of my Essential Self; a Self-Enjoyment I had lost at some point in my life, as veil after veil had come to shroud this Essence.

This Attraction increased as the Enjoyability of the "I" Feeling increased; an Enjoyability that, although I had never experienced it before in this life, was somehow, impossibly, Recognized, Remembered[29]. And as the Enjoyable Nature of the "I" Feeling increased, it came to have an increasing Gravitational Pull on Attention. I was both "moving toward", and being "pulled by".

And as Attention continued to merge like a drop into the Formless Ocean of the "I" Feeling… something happened.

Poof!

There was a realization (not really an adequate word), not simply of Mind, but across the Whole of my Being, that there was no answer to "what". For "I" could not be found, within, as an object, a "thing" to be described in objective terms. Thoughts like, "I am just Awareness." whispered from afar by the ever more faintly heard mind, were immediately met with more questions; "What, then, is Awareness? Is there a formless 'something' that is aware?" And that endless loop of questions finally brought me to a Profound Exhaustion; the futility of the question having brought even the now apparitional mind to the end of its utility. For there was no place in the fierce immediacy of this enquiry for theories or conjecture about what I was.

The last words uttered by the distant inner voice, verbalizing a Shock beyond my ability to express, were, "I… just… Am." And as

---

[29] Decades later I would hear Swami Lakshmanjoo, a Kashmir Shaivite teacher, say that when one first experiences what he called "God", there is a sense of remembrance.

The Journey to The Kingdom of Heaven

the last sound of "Am" ended in Awareness... "I" lost consciousness of everything, including myself, and yet... was not unconscious. "I" Remained as what I would later call Nonexistent Existence[30]. But make no mistake, this was not a vacuous, blank state or void. The Absolute Emptiness of all manifestation was not Empty.

> I have fainted several times in this life,
> And in that unconscious state,
> Awareness of everything ceased,
> Including awareness of myself.
>
> It was, in a sense, a death.
>
> Speaking of it after the fact,
> I can say that there was nothing,
> Not even myself aware of nothing,
> No knowledge of nonexistence...
>
> The very definition of unconscious.
>
> But I have Known another Fainting,
> When awareness of everything ceased,
> Including awareness of myself existing,
> And yet, I remained... as Existence.
>
> Speaking of it after the fact,
> I can say that there was nothing,
> Not even myself aware of nothing,
> And yet...

---

[30] A term I discovered in Sufism; the least problematic in describing what Hinduism calls Superconsciousness, and Christianity, Divine Union.

 An Affair of the Heart

> Awareness remained, aware of nothing,
> Existence remained, with nothing existing,
> Aliveness remained, with nothing alive,
> Creativity remained, with nothing created.
>
> The very definition of The Great Mystery.
>
> Something Wonderful, that is not a thing,
> Exists before the arising of all things,
> Something Wonderful, I had dreamed of,
> But could only Be in my vanishing.

All words are going to fail in describing the Experience of Nonexistent Existence, in which everything – space, time, all manifestation, all duality – Vanished Absolutely. Using words like "Awareness", "Aliveness" or "Consciousness" to describe what remained cannot help but imply something that is aware, alive, or conscious. Even my saying, in the previous sentence, "...'what' remained..." implies something that remained.

To this day the question of "What was that?!" remains the greatest Mystery, the most impossible-to-answer question. Throughout my life, after this Experience – and here we go again, as there was no experiencer – as I've perused scriptures seeking mention of it, hoping, in an act of futility, to gain some clarity, I've found nothing but interpretations, after the fact, by those who have experienced it. Each interpreter wrapped the Experience in the context of their cultures, religions, philosophies, and the place in time in which they existed. Some called it an experience of God, others called it the Self, others, Atman. All of these imply a formless something that exists prior to manifest reality. And whether that's so... I have no idea. Whatever remained had no sense of "itself" as a formless thing

The Journey to The Kingdom of Heaven

or otherwise. I just don't know what to say.

To say, as some teachers do, that in Nonexistent Existence, Awareness is aware only of itself, is not true of my Experience. For that implies a subtle subject-Awareness, aware of itself as the object of awareness, and that was not the case.

> Aliveness, Awareness, Existence,
> Before space, time, and objects;
>
> Not a theory, or a conclusion come to,
> But an Experience, had by no one.
>
> Aliveness, Awareness, Existence,
> Before the subject self, alive and aware;
>
> Not a theory, or a conclusion come to,
> But an Experience, had by no one.
>
> Aliveness, Awareness, Existence,
> Before the arising of *any* duality;
>
> Not a theory, or a conclusion come to,
> But an Experience, had by no one.
>
> Aliveness, Awareness, Existence,
> Not even aware of Itself as being aware;
>
> *All* duality, Vanished, *Absolutely*;
>
> Not a theory, or a conclusion come to,
> But an Experience, had by no one.

 An Affair of the Heart

> The Experience, without an experiencer,
> Of Nonexistent Existence.

There is no analog in our manifest experience, here in the realm of opposites, of manifest creation, in the experience of duality, for the nature of that Experience without an experiencer, that Experience of *Absolute* Nonduality.

But all of this is so analytical and clinical. What matters is not the technical description of the Experience, cherished by so many contemporary nondualists, but the Experiential nature.

The Unalloyed Ecstasy of Nonexistent Existence

Years later I would read scriptures that stated the Absolute as being without qualities or attributes. If that's so, then I did not Experience the Absolute. For there was a Quality that remained when all differentiated, dualistic qualities Vanished, when all duality, all polarities, vanished Absolutely. It was a Rapturous, Orgasmic Ecstasy that remained when the dualities of Ecstasy and Agony Vanished; an Ecstasy without opposite.

Words like Unalloyed Ecstasy[31] and Rapture are the closest we have. But these, like all words, are steeped in manifest connotations, and demean the nature of the Experience of our Essence; the "Am" before "I" am. It is an Experience worthy of the word "Heaven" – and I'm reminded, of course, of Jesus' words, "The Kingdom of Heaven is within." Not a place, but an Experience of, as the Sufis say, Nonexistent Existence. For the drop has fallen into the Ocean, into The Great Mystery, without the slightest trace of dropness

---

[31] From advaitic scripture.

The Journey to The Kingdom of Heaven

remaining. It is the answer to every prayer ever uttered, in all of eternity; the Fulfillment of the Heart's Desire.

Although there was no person present in Nonexistent Existence, what remained was the most Intimate of experiences… Me; what I Am. And, I suspect, what we all are in our Essence.

>   When we enter the Gates of Heaven,
>   Both "limited" and "limitless" vanish.
>
>   This is what is meant by "Infinite";
>   Not endless space,
>   But the vanishing of space, altogether.
>
>   When we enter the Gates of Heaven,
>   Past, future, and "now" vanish.
>
>   This is what is meant by "Eternal";
>   Not endless existence in time,
>   But the vanishing of time, altogether.
>
>   When we enter the Gates of Heaven,
>   The Enjoyer of Enjoyment vanishes.
>
>   This is what is meant by "Unalloyed Ecstasy";
>   Not endless pleasure had by an "experiencer",
>   But the vanishing of the experiencer, altogether.
>
>   When we enter the Gates of Heaven,
>   We vanish.

 An Affair of the Heart

This is what is meant by "Liberation";
Not the Benediction of "I",
But the vanishing of "I", altogether.

No space in which objects can arise.
No time in which objects can be perceived.

No objects to be perceived.
No subject-perceiver-experiencer,
To perceive, experience, cognize.

I did not feel myself expanded,
Existing as all of Creation,
For there was no "I",
And no Creation to expand into.

Nor did I feel myself as "That",
As "Consciousness", the Ground of Being,
Within which all of Creation arises,
And into which all Creation vanishes.

I did not feel myself… at all,
And yet, without existing, I Remained,
As Inexpressible Ecstasy,
Nonexistent, as Unmanifest Existence.

The Return

I have no idea how long, in manifest time, the Experience of Nonexistent Existence lasted. How could I possibly? But at some pointless point, in some timeless time, the Unmoving, Impenetrable Unicity was broken by the arising of an ever-so-very-subtle sense of

The Journey to The Kingdom of Heaven

subjectivity, of an experiencer, re-establishing individuation, and duality. In that first arising of individuated awareness, I was awash, still, in the Dissolution and Ecstasy of Nonexistent Existence, aware of myself only as that most-subtle of subjectivities I had experienced in the instant before Vanishing into and as Nonexistent Existence, when the inner voice had gasped, "I... just... Am!"

The Subtle Suffering
Inherent in Individuated Existence

In the instant when the first ever-so-subtle sense of subjectivity arose from the Experience of Nonexistent Existence, there was an instantaneous awareness of the Suffering inherent in individuated existence, a Suffering that was foundational, underlaying whatever other unease or pain might befall us in life. For the Rapture of Nonexistent Existence, the Fullness, Completion, and Ecstasy of the Heart's Desire Fulfilled, was, in that instant of time's arising, lost. Although still awash in that Ecstasy, it was diminished, no longer Absolute. For "I" was no longer Whole, having become, once again "I", a part; no longer Life Itself, but a thing alive. However imbued I remained with that Inexpressible Rapture[32], I Suffered, as we all do, from Separation[33]. But I was changed forever after, even in that Suffering.

The suffering inherent in individuated existence is something few of us become aware of in our life. We simply think it's what it feels like

---

[32] In my writing, I differentiate the Unalloyed "Ecstasy" of Nonexistent Existence from the "Bliss" of that Radiance, diminished in its arising in manifestation, but its Source unmistakable.

[33] I've always suspected that the Inherent Unease of individuated existence may be what Buddha meant by the term "Dukkha".

 An Affair of the Heart

to be alive. Only its juxtaposition to the Vanishing of All Suffering in Nonexistent Existence made it starkly apparent to me in the instant "I" was birthed again into manifest existence, into life as a thing existent, separate, individuated, among the infinite "other" things in manifest creation. You might say there was, across the whole of my manifest Being, in the instant of subjectivity's return, a Silent Groaning Sigh.

The Dense, Somatic Suffering Inherent in Personhood

In the moments following the arising of that first ever-so-subtle sense of subjectivity from Nonexistent Existence, the constituent aspects of manifest experience began to reappear, remembered with deepening depth and clarity, like a tide rolling into Awareness. I experienced a pre-verbal confoundment, initially, which eventually found words. And at some point, tragically and painfully, I remembered myself as a person; "who" I was, where I was, and all that that entailed. In the instant of returning to manifest existence, Nonexistent Existence had become a memory; a memory that could not be held in words, concepts, or inner imagery; a memory not of the relative kind, not of the mind, and yet, Remembered.

How could "I" Remember an Experience in which "I" was not present? An answer to this question escaped me for many years, until the obvious answer dawned on me one day; "I" am that which Remained when individuated I and all of manifest creation Vanished in Nonexistent Existence. I was, I am, we all are, Nonexistent Existence even as we are, in manifestation, the experience of embodied existence. Using Hindu terminology, we are Shiva, the

The Journey to The Kingdom of Heaven

unmanifest, and Shakti[34], the manifest; both being aspects of a Singularity, spoken of as two only for the sake of discussion. Using Sufi terminology, we are the Soul – that Inexplicable Juncture where the individuated expression of God meets the unindividuated, before God said, "Be." – and we are the Nafs, or individuated self. As I later discovered both of these perspectives, and others, as well, they seemed beautiful metaphors for my experience.

As the palpable, somatic sense of embodiment slowly but inexorably returned from Nonexistent Existence, the pain of personhood[35], being in such close juxtaposition to the Experience of Nonexistent Existence, was felt with an acuity I'd never before known. The initially subtle suffering of individuated existence was soon overwhelmed, in short order, by this more concrete and intense contraction across the whole of Being.

What I had experienced in the Absolute Dissolution Nonexistent Existence was beyond the Naked State of my earliest childhood; the experience I had sought so desperately. In fact, I had traversed through that state of painlessness on the way to The Kingdom of Heaven. The "normalcy" to which I had then returned was equivalent to being driven from the Garden of Eden.

I'm Here for You, Always

Still sitting in my nook, I burst into tears, and imagining Divine Mother before me, grabbed her around her calves, sobbing inwardly, "Why would you do this?! Why would you show me Heaven, only

---
[34] This is just one of the many uses of the word Shakti in Hinduism.
[35] The felt sense of personhood is, in my view, a condition, only delusionally felt as an actual entity.

An Affair of the Heart

to return me to this unbearable pain of separation?!"

In reading Yogananda's account of Master Mahasaya's relationship with Divine Mother, I'd related to the stance of child to mother. For I had always felt myself to be lacking those qualities and attributes that religion deemed requisite for Divine Revelation. The only hope, I felt, for one such as me, was the existence of a Divine Love that was uncaused and unconditional. And the image I held of a Divine Mother was of a Being who Loved me in that way, simply because I existed. Did I "believe" in a Divine Mother? Not at all. I had no verifiable evidence that such a Being existed. And yet, my Heart cried out to Her that day.

As I sat, clutching her calves, white-knuckled, sobbing, something remarkable happened. I heard the words, within, not arising from my own mind[36], "I am here for you, always, whether you're a good boy, or bad." But equally startling, as I heard those words, an Incredible Presence, a Powerful Force washed over the Whole of my Being, from my subtle body to the somatic; a palpable, visceral, energetic Force of Absolute Assurance. This was not simply an emotional response or reactivity within me. It was something that, like the voice, did not seem to originate from me.

My mind would later question this inner voice and energetic Assurance as simply an aberrant subjective experience, a self-hypnosis, however profound or "not of me" it may have seemed. This is the nature of the discriminating mind, and something to be respected and listened to, not dismissed. It is as it should be. My Heart, however, remained awash in the powerfully palpable Radiance of that Assurance, and releasing Her legs, inwardly, I sat

---

[36] This is impossible to describe accurately, and I don't blame anyone for thinking I simply said the words to myself.

The Journey to The Kingdom of Heaven

back, within, and soaked in the Absoluteness of an Assurance that was more Felt than heard. In the decades ahead, I would continue to doubt and test this Assurance again and again, only to have it be proven True, again and again, beginning the very day after this Experience. But… I'm getting ahead of myself.

I left the SRF gardens and returned home, full of Astounded, Lucid Confusion[37] at what had happened, and remained for the rest of that day awash in the Afterglow of the Ecstasy of Nonexistent Existence, of my own Essence.

---

[37] A phrase from Rumi.

 # An Affair of the Heart

The Inner Radiance

What if you found yourself,
Imbued always with a touch of Heaven,
Felt as a Radiance in the Locus of your Heart,
Sometimes the ambient background of experience,
Sometimes flooding the foreground, powerfully,
Ever available to the mind's Attention,
Ever available to the Heart's Remembrance…

A Wellspring, within, of Union's Dissolution and Ecstasy.

The day after the Experience at the SRF gardens I awoke as I had fallen asleep the night before, in a state of Astonished Wonderment. For what had happened the day before was real; not an impossible fairytale; not a hallucination or the product of hysterical imagining. It had really happened.

I assumed that the Experience the day before had been just that; an "experience", with a beginning and an end, that had come and gone. But its transience didn't trouble me. Whatever it was that had happened was profoundly life-changing, and I was happy and grateful simply to have had it, however finite its duration, and regardless of the fact that I had returned to manifest existence.

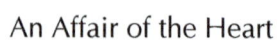 An Affair of the Heart

Coupled with the Experience of a week prior, I now lived with an Absolute certainty that there was more to life than meets the eye, and that The Heart's Desire could, in fact, be Fulfilled. The Impossible Dream I had longed for all my life was real, and was able to be Experienced not in a far off heaven, only by those who were "worthy", but here, while alive in manifest creation, and by one far from perfection. I Reveled in the Afterglow, in renewed Hope, renewed Inspiration, and renewed Aspiration.

But the Experience at the SRF gardens was *not* wholly transient.

The day after the Experience, I was driving down the coast highway and happened to pass the gardens. As I saw the golden lotus atop the arched entryway, I recalled what had happened the day before, and...

Before the mind's inner voice could utter a word as an aspect of the remembrance, I felt an Exquisite Ecstasy flooding my Being from the Locus of my Heart. It was the same Ecstasy I had Experienced in Nonexistent Existence, only diminished, no doubt due to its arising in manifest creation, in the experience of embodiment in the Dream of space, time, and objects. It burst like an explosion of Bliss in the center of my chest, like a Sun Brightening, but without center or periphery. And in the instant of its arising, inherent in that Ecstasy, dualistic perception became instantly more dissolute, and increasingly so as Wave after Wave washed over me, Flooding the whole of my Being. It felt as if I was starting to faint into the Experience of Nonexistent Existence.

In the instant of Remembrance, Attention had been pulled inward by the same powerful Gravity I had experienced the day before; back, behind, before. But this Experience, with eyes open, driving

The Inner Radiance

down the coast highway, was not, as it had been the day before, Absolute. Had it been, awareness of manifest creation, including myself, would have Vanished, and no doubt the car would have veered off the road disastrously. But although not Absolute, the Source of this Dissolution-Bliss was unmistakably the Essence I had Vanished into, and as, the day before. Fortunately, I was able to will Attention to the task of driving, even as the Exquisite Intoxication continued to wash through me.

The day before, the inward Journey of Attention had been effortful, requiring the relentless reassertion of fierce will, again and again, against the outward gravitational pull of powerful habituated tendencies. But now, in simply Remembering[38], I was instantaneously Greeted from within by The Inner Radiance, by Dissolution and Bliss, and pulled effortlessly by an inward Gravity into ever-deepening Absorption.

> In Remembrance, we are not asleep,
> And yet, we abandon the world,
> Our many cares within it, and ourself.
>
> In Remembrance, we are not dead,
> And yet, we abandon our life, our self,
> Surrendering to Exquisite Oblivion.
>
> In Remembrance, is a forgetting,
> Of all but The Beloved's Face,
> In which world and self are no more.

---

[38] The term I would use for some time after, to describe the Experience of Attention's inward turning, whether by remembering, myself, or being Remembered spontaneously, out of nowhere.

 An Affair of the Heart

> Be of good cheer, do not despair,
> At the Vanishing of the world, created,
> And yourself, created, a part of it.
>
> For in the End of all things is revealed,
> What imagination cannot conceive,
> That no longer existing, you Remain…
>
> In the Heaven of Nonexistent Existence,
> The Fulfillment of the Heart's Desire,
> The Answer to every prayer uttered…
>
> The rememberer, Forgotten.

In the hours and days that followed, I discovered that this Inner Radiance, as I came to call it, was ever-available to Remembrance. This was not a Remembrance of an Experience had previously, that had come and gone, but of a Living Presence[39], ever-available Here and Now; the Experience of my own Ecstatic Essence; a Presence that would prove, again and again, and to this day, to be "Here for me, Always," just as Divine Mother[40] had assured.

It was as if the Experience of Nonexistent Existence had somehow poked a hole in Heaven, and a River of that Unmanifest Ocean had begun flowing, impossibly, into manifest experience, Subsuming Attention, Intoxicating and Illumining my Being here, in form, from the Formless Unmanifest. All I needed to do was Remember, and

---

[39] Early on, after the Experience that defined his spiritual life, the Hindu saint Ramana Maharshi used the term "avasam", or possession, to describe the Presence that became his ongoing Experience. Only later, after being exposed to advaita, did he begin using advaitic terminology.

[40] One of many terms I came to use, including The Beloved, The Beautiful One, to express both the Absolute Ecstasy of Nonexistent Existence, and Dissolution-Bliss, that Ecstasy's diminished arising in manifestation.

The Inner Radiance

the Flame of Dissolution-Ecstasy[41] Brightened, Flooding Experience. I suspect it may be what the Sufis refer to as Drunkenness on the Wine of The Beloved; The Tavern of The Beloved being my own Heart, where The Beautiful One has taken up Residence.

In struggling to describe The Inner Radiance to friends, I find often used words such as peace, happiness, joy, or wellbeing to be wholly inadequate. For the only phrase I have found that comes even remotely close to describing both the Experience of Nonexistent Existence and The Inner Radiance is "Spiritually Orgasmic".

I understand that for some, this metaphor is troubling, bringing to mind gross physicality. But that is not at all what I mean. I simply mean that just as a physical orgasm is not what you would call a peaceful, happy, joyful experience, but a momentary Absorption in what is our most rapturous physical pleasure; a brief moment in which both lover and beloved vanish in an experience of exquisite singularity; even so, the Experience of our Essence is Rapturous, only Spiritually so, to a degree and with a Singular Quality for which there are no adequate analogs in manifest, relative experience. It is an Ecstasy without opposite, only arising in the vanishing of duality.

In addition to the Ecstatic nature of The Inner Radiance, there is a feeling of Absolute Fullness and Completion. Fullness without opposite; nothing can be added or taken away. Completion without opposite; all movement of seeking, of grasping for more, has ceased. The word "wellbeing" is a far distant cousin of the Warmth and Richness inherent in The Inner Radiance.

When I use phrases such as, "The Wellspring of The Heart,"

---

[41] In my experience, Ecstasy is not an "effect" of Dissolution. The two are inseparable, each an inherent aspect of the other, like wetness to water, or heat to fire.

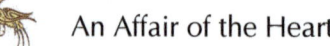 An Affair of the Heart

"The Garden of The Beloved," or "The Tavern of The Beloved", I am referring, metaphorically, to both the formless nature of the Experience of Nonexistent Existence, and to the welling up of Dissolution-Bliss in manifest embodiment; an impossible to describe Experience of the Transcendent having become, impossibly, immanent.

A friend once asked, "Without spiritual desire, how will you ever become fully Self Realized?" My answer was that whether I was Blessed or cursed in this condition, it was as it was, for the Desire for more was nowhere to be found, within, nor could I rekindle it, for only ash remained of the terrible thirst born of separation, and the desperate desire for its quenching.

> If there is more, here,
> Where the Path has vanished,
> She will have to carry me to it,
> For She has crept into my Heart,
> And stolen the lack, the emptiness,
> That moved me along The Way.
>
> In its place, the Beloved Thief,
> Left a piece of Her Heart in mine,
> And I cannot move, Intoxicated,
> With the Beautiful Perfume,
> Of Her Fullness, Completion, and Bliss.
>
> I read the other day of great danger,
> In becoming trapped at any juncture,
> Along the Way to Heaven,
> And could only smile at my misfortune,
> The Beautiful Thief's most tragic Gift.

The Inner Radiance

For what am I to do now?
How will I ever become "enlightened",
While I remain Drunk at Her Tavern,
Outside the door of which…
No Path is to be found?

How can I be Hungry,
When I am Full?
How can I be Thirsty,
When I Drown in Her Wine?
How can I care for attainment,
When I rest in the Arms,
Of Love without condition?

If there is more,
Here, where the Path has vanished
She will have to carry me to it,
Or bring it to me, through Grace,
For I am hobbled, faint,
Besotted in the Ecstasy,
Of Her Loving Embrace.

Pour me another, my Love,
Your Face is my Heaven.
And as you touch my Heart,
And hand me the Cup,
Let us toast the end of Suffering,
And the advent of that Love…
In which Lover and Beloved Vanish.

If there is more, I care nothing for it.

 An Affair of the Heart

Make no mistake, peripheral desires remained which might be deemed "spiritual", at least regarding the confounded mind. For it continued to wonder, as is its nature, what it was that had happened at the SRF gardens, and what it was that lingered, now, at the Heart of Being. But such questions arose, now, from Curiosity, rather than desperate need. For my lack of intellectual understanding, of concepts, words, or images to describe, did not in any way diminish The Inner Radiance, which remained, and remains, a Mystery, within; just as Nonexistent Existence remained, and remains to this day, a Mystery.

As I went on to explore the various traditions in the hope of finding some context for my Experience(s) within the experiences of others, I found similarities in their various descriptions of such experiences, but also found disparities between their theologies. My mind continued to wonder at the existence of God, in some form or other, and to wonder at the nature of manifest existence. Indeed, more questions arose to the mind than ever before, each apparent answer birthing more questions in an ever-flowing, ever-widening river of, "What?! Why?! How?!" But at the Heart of Being... there was no river; only The Ocean.

> We're older now, Mind and Heart,
> With less ahead of us, than behind.
> All our lives we have wondered,
> At this Great Matter of... Existing.
> This Great Matter of Being Alive.

The Inner Radiance

In our wanderings, far and wide,
We have spent time in the walled villages,
Of many traditions, many teachings.
Villages laid out this way and that,
In their expressions of "truth", "reality"…

And "enlightenment".

In each village Mind has run,
Like a starving vagrant, malnourished,
To the temples of knowledge,
To sit at the feet of the "enlightened",
Gorging voraciously…

On interpretations and descriptions,

While the Heart, having none of it,
Reveled in Bliss at the Tavern of The Beloved,
Sipping Grace, as She poured, again and again,
Until all was forgotten,
And only She and Heart remained…

Then… both Vanishing.

Each time, in the village of each tradition,
Mind would arrive, in time, at the Tavern door,
Bedraggled, forlorn, more ignorant than before.
And there, joining Heart at the bar,
Would sob to all who would listen, its tale of woe.

   An Affair of the Heart

>And in time, each time, again and again,
>The two staggering drunkards, Mind and Heart,
>Pushed open the village gates and wandered out;
>The Heart… into Endless Wonder,
>The mind…
>
>Into the Incomprehensibility of This Great Mystery

Illumination with The Inner Radiance did not rid me of the lesser self, transmuting me into a perfected Being. Nor did it vanquish The Great Suffering or Existential Fear. It did not bring an end to the ever-changing weather, often painful and heartbreaking, of psychology and emotion. Nor did it dissolve the samskaras and vasanas accumulated over a lifetime, though some appeared to diminish. It did not remove the felt sense of personhood; bondage to the mechanism of self-referencing that had created, then sustained, the felt sense of my personal self. Rather, all of those "Peripheral" aspects of manifest Being co-existed with The Radiance that Shone, untouched, unmoved, and impenetrable by those perturbations, in the Deepest Interiority of my Being.

A Vision

The Sea will be the Sea,
Whatever the drop's philosophy
-Farid ud-Din Attar

When I originally wrote this chapter, my Hindu friends were celebrating Navratri; nine days in which the various aspects of the Divine Mother are worshipped. In my own way of celebrating the Mystical nature of life, I offer this true story which, although involving a Hindu Goddess, refers, in my Heart, not to any religion in particular, but to the Great Mystery that transcends all such differentiations.

> If you come for tea and sweets, my Muslim friend,
> Don't leave in a huff if you see upon my wall,
> The picture of a Hindu Goddess smiling.
>
> If you come to sit in fellowship, my Christian friend,
> Don't curl your lip at the Moorish lanterns,
> The books of Hafez, Sanai, and Attar strewn about.

 An Affair of the Heart

> If you come for the porch's soft breeze, my Buddhist friend,
> Don't dismiss me as a deluded deist when tears well up,
> As I gaze at the Christian monstrance.
>
> My house, my Heart, my Life,
> Is a Wine of many grapes, but One Vintner,
> A Garden of many Roses, but One Gardener.
>
> "I profess the religion of Love," said Ibn Arabi,
> "Wherever its caravan turns along the way,
> That is the belief, the faith I keep."
>
> And so it will be with you and me,
> My friends of many faiths,
> If you come for tea.

Let me preface this by saying that those who know me will attest I am a fiercely rational, empirically-minded man, not a hysterical religionist, or one given over to wild "imaginings". I'm confident this true story will send certain of my friends fleeing. But it is one of the most significant, and confounding, experiences of my spiritual life.

I know that some of my "nondual" friends will dismiss this, and I understand their reasoning. But it happened. I know that some of my friends who adhere to a particular faith might be put off, because the vision was in the context of Hinduism. I can only ask the forbearance of my friends of many faiths. Please try to see beyond the Hinduness, and think of it as I do; that the religious context of the image had only to do with the vehicle available in that moment. For if there is a relational aspect to The Great Mystery, it is not of any particular faith, ethnicity, or culture. That, to me, seems simply obvious.

A Vision

In Hinduism, Brahma is the god who brings all of creation into being, Vishnu is the god who brings creation to fruition and sustains it all, and Shiva is the god of its eventual dissolution. These "masculine" gods represent the transcendent aspects of their respective functions; formless, unmanifest potentiality. But each has a "feminine" consort, or Shakti, which represents the manifest aspect; the energy, the impulse that moves that unmanifest potentiality into manifest form, and enlivens it there.

And so, let's begin.

It was 1983. I was sitting in the living room at the house of some friends, waiting for them to get ready to go with me to a movie. I sat on the couch, looking at a poster of the goddess Lakshmi hanging above their fireplace. Lakshmi is the consort, or shakti, of Vishnu. After gazing at the poster for some time, the room slowly filled, to my amazement, with that most remarkable, translucent Light; a light so Beautiful, so Exquisite, being not quite golden and not quite white. This was the same Light I had seen when meditating with my first teacher. The Light was not physical, of course, not in the physical space of the room. As was the case when meditating with that teacher, when I blinked, the Light was still there. My entire field of vision became subsumed in this Light, and the clearly defined features of the objects in the room began to dissolve into it. In the vague perception of objects that remained, it was as if everything had become "molten" gold. And eventually, all differentiation vanished in the Radiance of that Light.

All the while, my gaze remained upon the beautiful goddess in the poster. And a remarkable aspect of this vision is that the poster, unlike all else in the field of vision, and although Illumined with that beautiful Light, was not diffused, was not dissolving into that field.

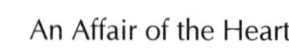 An Affair of the Heart

Again, such had been the case when meditating with the teacher; only he remained clearly defined in the field of Light emanating from him. And, as when meditating with the teacher, Lakshmi became more sharply defined, in an effect I would later come to call 6D, for it was somehow more clear, sharp, and pristine than anything I had experienced in dimensionality. Equally remarkable, the borders of the poster now encompassed a living world, for the goddess and the background all became inexpressibly dimensional.

I cannot remember when it occurred, or how, but at some point She was no longer in the poster, but standing, life-size, in the middle of the room, five or so feet in front of me, a few feet above where the ground would have been, had it not been subsumed in that Light. Her life-size form remained beautifully articulated in 6D, Illumined Radiantly.

Her blue sari became a blue I had never perceived, and Her golden jewelry dazzled and shimmered, again, like nothing I had ever seen. But most incredibly, She appeared to be... Alive, not only dimensional. She was the embodiment of, and emanated the Essence of the most Exquisite Beauty, Pristine Excellence, Fruition, Perfection, and... well, there is no describing the fullness of Her qualities.

I sat for some time, transfixed by this astounding, Transcendent Beauty, this impossible dimensionality, and then... She changed. In a transmutation I cannot describe, she became Vishnu. This was not a vague, hallucinatory morphing, for Vishnu was distinctly different than Lakshmi, equally dimensional, equally pristine in sharpness and clarity, and covered in shimmering golden armor, imbued with that Beautiful light. Although masculine, He did not appear to be

A Vision

a man, for the Radiance that emanated from Him had nothing of humanness in it. He emanated all of the qualities of Lakshmi, but there was a difference; a difference that I can only sum up in one word: Victory.

I sat for some time, transfixed, and then… He changed, becoming Lakshmi again.

Just like the field of vision, the sense of time had become diffused, as had the sense of space, as had the sense of myself as the perceiver, the experiencer of this vision, for I had lost all sense of myself as an object-perceiver-experiencer-person. And yet, all that I describe was appearing.

Several times this transmutation occurred; Lakshmi to Vishnu, Vishnu to Lakshmi. And then, the single most remarkable aspect of this vision occurred. For Lakshmi, who had thus far been gazing straight ahead, as she appeared in the physical poster, slowly turned Her head to me, and abandoning Her Expression of Sublime, Transcendent Repose, smiled Lovingly, nodded Her head down, then lifted it up, and slowly turned forward again.

Shortly thereafter, the vision ended, and everything returned to "normal".

I had not been alone in the room. A friend had been sitting near me on the couch, paging through a magazine to bide the time. I assumed the vision had been my own, and that while I had been lost in the incredible experience, he had simply carried on, unaware. I didn't mention the vision to him, partly because it didn't feel right to do so, but also because I was still dazed, not quite "myself", awash in that Radiance, Intoxicated.

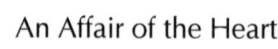 An Affair of the Heart

But then... my friend turned to me and asked, "Did you see that?" A bit shaken, I asked, "Did I see what?" And with his own expression of astonishment, he said, "Lakshmi turned, smiled, and nodded Her head."

In the Afterglow of the vision I was not in a state that would allow the mind to jump in and begin making something of this. I was utterly nonplussed. I think that as much as, if not more than the experience itself, I was now astonished by the fact that my friend had seen it, too, and described it to me before I had told him what I'd seen. It would have been a remarkable experience had it been confined to my subjectivity. But my friend having seen it; that took the whole affair to another level. For my rational, empirical mind, considering the Vision after the fact, would not be able to dismiss or diminish it as merely a subjective "hallucination", however shockingly vivid and lucid it may have been.

Not long after the Vision passed, and my friend's revelation, our friends came into the living room, with no idea of what had happened, lively and chattering, ready to head out to the movie. Nether my friend nor I said a word to them of the Vision. And although it may seem odd, I don't recall us speaking much to each other of it again, until I sent him this story recently for validation.

It was 35 years after this Vision that, remembering it one day, a remarkable aspect of the experience dawned on me; something that, astonishingly, I simply hadn't recognized with such clarity or impact before: the turning of Her head, the smiling, and the bowing of Her head... these were acts of volition, gestures of a sentient Being! This recognition gave new impetus to the questions that have confounded my mind since the Vision, to this very day. Who? What? Why?

A Vision

As I write, it's been 39 years or so since the Vision, and I've still no idea what to make of it. My friends of various faiths each see it through the prism of their respective beliefs. But I remain in utter confoundment. The Vision didn't inform me about any theology, didn't describe the nature of "reality", or explain a divine plan. It didn't tell me what it meant, how I was supposed to relate to such a Being, or what, if anything, I was supposed to do as a consequence. It remains perhaps the single greatest mystery of my life.

To this day I naturally live in wonder at the Experience of Nonexistent Existence, as I do regarding The Inner Radiance. But in my old age I'm not as compelled as I was in the past to know the "what", "why", and "wherefore" of these. But this Vision…

An Affair of the Heart

A Period of Divine Madness

*"If you must be Mad,
Be Mad for God"*
-Ramakrishna

After the Experience at SRF and the subsequent advent of The Inner Radiance, I went on to be in a spiritual relationship with my first teacher. The experiences I had during my time with him rolled over me like a tsunami, sweeping away my old life, and sweeping me away into a new one I could never have imagined; a life that in time would take on a certain extraordinary ordinariness, but initially was anything but. In those early days, every moment, every breath, every heartbeat was filled with Powerful Mystical Promise, and that promise was the sole matter of my consideration. How could it be otherwise, given all that had happened?

This teacher taught a theory expressed in various traditions, that there is a point in each of our lives where those of us who are spiritually inclined, awaken. Not in the sense of "awakening" as the term is so often used these days, with its implied finality, but a time when the bud cracks open, exposing the delicate petals to sunlight for the first time; the beginning of an acceleration in spiritual unfoldment. After

 An Affair of the Heart

this initial cracking open comes a period of blossoming into flower, and for some, fruition.

After the Experience of Nonexistent Existence and the advent of The Inner Radiance there was a period of months in which I was quite Mad with Inspiration and Aspiration. It was a period of first Love, spiritually speaking, in which I dared to hope that so much of what I'd hoped for and dreamed of, spiritually, might possibly be true, and might possibly come to fruition in my own direct experience.

I had been shown – not conceptually, but experientially – that existence was a matter of unimaginable Wonder, that even seemingly mundane "reality" was a Mystical affair, and that the spiritual world I had hoped against all hope to be real was not a fairytale for the simple-minded or hysterically religious, but as actual as the solid reality with which I'd become so familiar and comfortable, and had previously taken to be all that existed.

My Madness was not based on the memory of a past spiritual experience that had come and gone, for The Inner Radiance was Alive at the Heart of my Being, and a continual Wonder, Reminder, and Enticement. In Hindu terms, the Bliss of the Atman Shone unobscured, within. In Sufi terms, The Beloved had taken up residence in the Secret Garden of my Heart, and Her Perfume surrounded me. In Christian terms, The Holy Spirit was a Living Presence, within.

For many months during the first year after the experience of Nonexistent Existence, during each meditation with my first teacher, the outer world would dissolve in that Exquisitely Beautiful translucent Light I had seen the first time I had meditated with him; or, I should say, been "meditated" with him. Attention would

A Period of Divine Madness

dissolve into the Rapturous Inner Radiance, and tears of Wonder, Awe, and Gratitude would stream down my face. It was during this period that many of the miraculous events described in the chapter, "Mystical Experiences With my First Teacher" occurred, and more, including the Vision of Lakshmi and Vishnu.

In those early years, it was Hinduism that captured my Heart, and the context into which I poured my Experience(s). Part of this had to do with the fact that my first teacher taught an Americanized form of Hinduism. But it also had much to do with my having read *Autobiography of a Yogi*, early on, and later having become deeply infatuated with, *The Gospel of Ramakrishna*. For someone who didn't believe in any of the conventionally accepted notions of God(s), Christian, Hindu, or otherwise, I was deeply engaged, in those early years, with the notion of the Divine Mother that I'd read of in *The Gospel of Ramakrishna*. I held a deep affinity with the devotional nature of Ramakrishna's relationship to the Great Mystery, for mine, too, was the stance of a helpless child.

It was, after all, Divine Mother who I had called out to that day at the SRF gardens, pleading, "How could you be so cruel?!" And it was Divine Mother whose legs I grabbed in desperation when the world of manifest creation reappeared from Nonexistent Existence, and who assured me, "I am here for you, Always." And it was Divine Mother, in the form of the Hindu goddess Lakshmi, who had turned, smiled, and nodded during the Vision.

My mind continued to do its job, questioning these things as possibly nothing more than imaginings – though it could not dismiss the Vision, which had been empirically verified. But my Heart longed for Relationship with whatever it was that had appeared to me and which I felt possessed the Heart of my Being as The Inner Radiance,

An Affair of the Heart

which I also felt, confoundingly, to be my own Essence. Although this period was short-lived, for several reasons, a bit of that Madness remains always with me. For The Inner Radiance cares nothing for my inspiration or lack thereof, my belief or disbelief, my faith or lack thereof. And its Presence is, by normal standards, the source of an ongoing Madness.

Mystical Experiences with My First Teacher

Life is the craziest experience I've ever had.
-the author

There was a time when I deemed the Experiences I've described thus far in this book as "Magical". For they were outside of anything I had known; outside of what I deemed "real" or even possible. But in time, as I continued to Experience an Illumined Heart, and all else that unfolded, I came to see Existence itself as one continuous Mystical Experience, accentuated by occasional Experiences of uncommon significance, indicating arrival at different milestones along The Way.

The Mystical thoroughly permeated my moment-to-moment existence. And when I considered it all in juxtaposition to the perspective of my earlier life, it indeed seemed quite mad. Mad, in the sense that I did not understand much of anything regarding the Nature of existence, much less Mystical Experiences or Transmuting Milestones arrived at. Mad, in the sense that I truly did feel myself a stranger in the strangest of lands; the ordinary having become

 An Affair of the Heart

extraordinary, the secular having become sacred. Mad in the sense that the circle of those I could speak with of these things had become smaller and smaller, even among my first teacher's community.

In the decades since these early experiences, the mind has come to realize that it will never come to the clarity it seeks, in the way it seeks. And yet it continues, as is its nature, to be moved by the desire to know and understand. After all this time, I continue to live in a state of Wonder and… Not Knowing.

> I know Nothing,
> I understand Nothing,
> I am unaware of Myself,
> I am in Love,
> But with whom I do not know.
> -Farid ud-Din Attar

I'm including the following anecdotes because they continue to be points of fascination for me and, if you accept the possibility that I'm not delusional, may help shake you into fascination and open-mindedness, as well, if you are not already so. As with all that's occurred, I don't really know what to make of these Experiences. They are simply fascinating mysteries that put a special sparkle on the Experience of life, and declare, as I've said so often thus far, that there's more to life than meets the eye.

Meditations

As time passed, meditations with my first teacher continued to be Mystical experiences, just as the first meditation had been, and in certain ways, even more so. In each meeting, The Inner Radiance

Mystical Experiences with My First Teacher

would begin welling up before he even arrived[42]. He would speak briefly, then close his eyes and begin meditating. We kept our eyes open, keeping a loose gaze upon his form. Always there was that impossible-to-explain golden-white Light filling the room, emanating from his form. Often everything in the field of vision would vanish into that Light, and only the image of the teacher would remain, visible in the startling clarity I called 6D. Always, The Inner Radiance welled up with even greater intensity during meditations, dissolving dualistic experience and flooding my being with the Ecstasy of that Dissolution.

At some point he would open his eyes, still deeply absorbed, and one by one, spend time meditating on each of us, looking directly at us. When he would reach me, almost always sitting in the back of the hall, any lingering objects in the field of vision, long since diffused in Light, vanished utterly, and only his 6D form remained. This Light, of course, was not in the physical room. The intensity and depth of my own Dissolution and Bliss would become near overwhelming. When he would move on, the vague, diffused-in-Light forms in the room might reappear, but still covered in that molten golden Light.

After meditations, I would remain in an altered state for several days; a state similar to the experience I'd known after that first meditation with him. As the days passed, I would feel "normal" awareness slowly reasserting itself. I discovered that this was the common experience of others who were in relationship with this teacher. It was as if we had been immersed in an Ocean of Radiance, and remained wet upon emerging, slowly drying over several days.

---

[42] See the story "Your Crown Chakra's Glowing!"

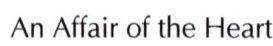 An Affair of the Heart

The Inner Radiance, however, while Brightening dramatically during the meditations, neither increased nor decreased in the days following the meditation, unless, of course, I chose to let Attention Dissolve into it, or was spontaneously solicited. Rather, it was my energetic and psychological states that were altered for those few days after meditations.

The Yantra Throwing Meditation

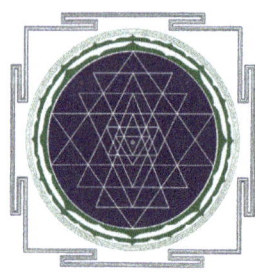

Throughout the time with my first teacher, and throughout my entire life, really, I repeatedly came into conflict with the notion of "practice" and the notion of doing something, or refraining from doing something, in order to arrive at a conditional state. For reasons that I don't understand to this day, I didn't see, then, that I was predominantly devotional by nature.

Since reading Yogananda's description of his time with Master Mahasaya, and then reading *The Gospel of Ramakrishna*, I had been in a tenuous relationship with the notion of a Divine Mother. That is why on that fateful day at SRF, after cursing everyone from Jesus, to Buddha, and every other saint or God I could recall, my rage subsided when I cried out to Her, "How could You be so cruel?"

Techniques and practice to attain the "goal" of Mother's Love made me recoil. And because my first teacher recommended a specific method of meditation, I was an utter failure at regular practice. It seemed that whenever I sat "formally" to meditate, The Inner Radiance would suddenly move far away from me. The moment

Mystical Experiences with My First Teacher

I would relax, and stop "doing" meditation, it would be Present, even welling up, almost in response to that relaxing of effort. It was as if that Radiance was somehow volitional, and was teaching me something through its brightening or dimming[43].

But holding the teacher to be wiser than myself, not yet trusting my own experience or intuition, and moved largely by guilt, I would try, every once in a while, to do as he recommended. And so, one morning I dragged myself dejectedly to my meditation table, and lit the incense and candles in front of the Sri yantra[44]. As I sat there, I thought, "OK, now I'll focus here for a while, then shift focus there for a while; concentration, then letting go. Then, if I'm able to concentrate perfectly, then maybe, only maybe, might I begin to feel whatever everyone meant by "meditation."

It seemed so cruel that Mother's Love was held hostage to techniques and gestures. As I sat there, in my mind I saw a house behind the darkness of my closed eyes. But a wall surrounded the house, and at the gate stood a fierce guard. Within the house was my Mother, my very own, my nearest and dearest. This was my house, my home. But the guard refused to allow me entry because I had not yet learned to concentrate perfectly, had not yet learned to let go properly, had not yet become virtuous enough, had not yet accrued sufficient merit, had not yet gained any number of prerequisites for entry.

What was this?! "Mother!!!" I cried, inwardly, defiant. I began crying uncontrollably. I hurled the yantra across the room in rage, and collapsed on the floor in sorrow, sobbing breathlessly, "Mother, how could you be so cruel?! How could you be so cruel!" I could

---
[43] For the most striking example of this "teaching", see the story "Little Monkey".
[44] A geometric design used to aid the type of meditation taught by my first teacher.

An Affair of the Heart

barely breath, I could not move. I vanished into a samadhi of pure despair.

After crying desperately for some time, I simply kept my eyes closed, and lay there. I did not have the strength to rise, or the desire to face this dilemma again. There seemed no hope of resolution between my inner attitude and the notion of striving and attainment.

Eventually I sat up… and only then realized that as I had laid there in despair, crying to Mother, my consciousness had been transmuted. It was as if I was not myself anymore. I felt an inexpressible love for…myself, except, I was not myself anymore. I saw the yantra across the room. "Oh, my dearest," I whispered. I saw a pair of sneakers in the open closet. It was his closet, and those were his shoes. And the sight of them, because they were his, filled me with a Love that I cannot capture in words. I walked over and picked them up lovingly. They were precious to me, because they were his. I began crying out of Love, and said, inwardly, "These are his shoes!" Later, I stood in the kitchen, and watched a pot of water boil, enamored with the whole affair. He was boiling water. "This is his house. These are his friends!"

I do not mean to say that I became Divine Mother. But for a time I saw through Her eyes, and felt through her Heart. Such Boundless, Inexpressible Love for Her son. I will not continue to try, fruitlessly, to describe this state of awareness. It lasted for several days, diminishing gradually as they passed.

Mystical Experiences with My First Teacher

A Special Day in Eternity

My first teacher recommended meditating twice a day, but as I've explained, I seldom did. In spite of my inherent aversion, one Sunday I succeeded in dragging myself to the meditation table in the morning. After overcoming my usual resistance, I noticed that The Inner Radiance was welling up with an uncommon intensity, taking my breath away. I quickly reached a state where I was deeply immersed in an Ocean of Deep and Powerful Bliss, verging on the Ecstasy of Nonexistent Existence. It was as if there was an actual velocity to the inward sinking, a powerful gravitational pull exerted from within. Because the meditation was so effortless, the Dissolution of dualistic awareness so powerful, and its nature so Exquisitely Blissful, I stayed sitting for 2 1/2 hours. Something clearly auspicious was going on.

Days later, in a casual conversation with a friend who'd been at my first teacher's home over the weekend, I learned that on Sunday he had mentioned that day to have been, "A special day in Eternity."

This is the Last Lifetime

Not long after I began study with my first teacher, he sat in a half-lotus on a table at the front of a hall. He had just begun meditating. I was sitting three rows from the front, and to his left. As always, we meditated with our eyes open, keeping a loose gaze on him. And as always, the room filled with that translucent gold-white Light, and as happened in each meditation, all were Transported.

This meditation took place during my period of Spiritual Madness, when inspiration, aspiration, and hope were unrestrained, and

An Affair of the Heart

in their full glory. But in the course of this particular meditation I became suddenly discouraged and impatient. For although Illumined with The Inner Radiance, I still suffered from the terrible contraction of personal identity. I felt such inner desperation, and in keeping with my petulant nature, experienced concurrent sorrow and rage at the fact that I still suffered so. For nothing that I did, or refrained from doing, seemed to alleviate the suffering of "myself". The Inner Radiance did not seem to be dissolving that salt doll.

As the meditation continued, I found myself drowning in frustration and anger, and I screamed inwardly with all my Being, "I WANT MY FREEDOM!!!" I watched in amazement as the teacher opened his eyes, turned his head, and looked directly at me, meditating upon me for some time. I was blinded by that Radiant, translucent Light. My mind stopped, dualistic awareness became dissolute, and I was Immersed in the Ecstasy of my Essence, which welled up powerfully, almost completely subsuming my individuated awareness.

He then turned his head back, looking forward once again, closing his eyes in meditation. I was nonplussed. Had he heard my inner cry? Was such a thing possible? My inherent skepticism would not be stilled or quieted.

But soon, awash in Dissolution and Bliss, I forgot what had happened. And again, in the midst of this Ecstatic state, I found myself suddenly lost in frustration, despair, and anger, demanding, screaming inwardly a second time, "I WANT MY FREEDOM!!!" And again, to my absolute astonishment, the teacher opened his eyes, turned his head, and gazed directly at me. And again, I was Taken, unable even to think of the incredible nature of what had just happened. For a second time, it seemed, impossibly, this man had heard my inner cry? After some time he turned his head back,

Mystical Experiences with My First Teacher

looking forward once again, and closed his eyes in meditation.

I don't know how it's possible that this twice-occurring miracle did not silence my skepticism, but it did not. I again returned to meditation, and again, although Immersed in Dissolution and Bliss, eventually found myself frustrated, impatient, and enraged at the bondage to personhood. And again the ferocity of the energy accompanying that inner desperation made me unable to restrain myself from inwardly screaming yet a third time, with even more passion than the previous times, "I… WANT… MY… *FREEDOM!!!*" And yet again, the teacher opened his eyes, turned his head, and gazed directly at me. And yet again, I was Taken. And after some time, he returned again to looking forward, closing his eyes in meditation.

He meditated for quite some time longer. At the end of meditations, he never spoke immediately, but with eyes opened, remained Dissolute for some time, as we all did. Eventually he would begin speaking, but only after this gentle re-emergence into manifest experience.

But this time he finished the meditation, opened his eyes, turned to look directly at me, and said several things. Of those several things, I remember only bits and pieces; "Don't be concerned with your ups and downs. Don't be concerned with power. The script for this play, in which we are all players, was written long ago." He then paused, and said, "This is the last lifetime."

Later, in higher moments, remembering the statement regarding the last lifetime would fill me with inspiration, for it implied enlightenment, whatever that meant, would occur at some point in this lifetime. But in moments of frustration, impatience, and

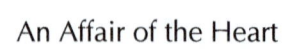 An Affair of the Heart

despair, the statement made me crazy, as the end of inner suffering seemed an utter impossibility. Again and again, I would forget his admonition not to be concerned with my ups and downs.

I wasn't concerned with reincarnation or not returning to manifest existence. All of that was mere theory to me. I wanted freedom from the felt sense of my personal self and its attendant suffering. But that felt sense would only become more painful, more acutely dense for decades to follow, until one day, it would in fact suddenly Vanish. But… that's a later chapter.

Your Crown Chakra's Glowing!

I was at a public meditation for my first teacher at an old, ornate theatre; a large hall, holding hundreds of people. There were two aisles, dividing three sections of seating. I was sitting near the front, off to one side, close to the wall, far from the aisle. The teacher hadn't yet arrived, and I was sitting there meditating. Suddenly the person next to me nudged my shoulder to get my attention, and pointed to the aisle. A man was standing there leaning into the row in which I was sitting. He shouted, "Are you meditating?" I nodded yes. He shouted, "My girlfriend and I are sitting in the back, and we both saw your crown chakra glowing."

I didn't know what to say.

It's Got Nothing to do with That

One of the locations where my first teacher held meditations was in a beach community near Los Angeles, only blocks from the beach. He'd only recently started meditations there, and many of the new

Mystical Experiences with My First Teacher

students had yet to learn the spiritual etiquette that was an essential part of that teacher's teaching.

When I first began meditating with this teacher, there remained traditional strands of orthodoxy in the somewhat Americanized version of Hinduism he taught. Men and women attended separate meetings, so that each could focus more easily on spirituality, without the inevitable distractions of the opposite sex. And during my period of Spiritual Madness, I actually appreciated this arrangement, for as Mad as I was for spirituality, I remained, at the same time, mad for romance and physicality. But things had changed from those early days, and we were now co-educational. And to those of us who were earlier students, with a more orthodox bent, those in the Los Angeles community were notorious for their bohemian approach to spirituality and lack of spiritual etiquette. I often commented sarcastically that compared to the San Diego center, the Los Angeles center was like a brothel. Calling it a nightclub would have been a more balanced assessment, but this just goes to show how orthodox I was, in some ways, during my brief period of spiritual Madness.

Most notorious in the Los Angeles community was one young woman in particular, Valerie, who was notorious for her provocative attire. My own introduction to her, however, proved a miraculous event.

One evening at this location, I was standing at the door of the hall where the meditation was about to take place, talking with friends, when a beautiful young woman entered the hall, wet from head to toe, wearing only shorts and a halter top. She had evidently just come from a dip in the nearby ocean. Rolling his eyes, one of the friends said, "Oh, that's Valerie." We were amazed. How could someone be so unaware?

 An Affair of the Heart

When it was time for the meeting to begin, I found a seat in the back, where I usually sat. The seats to my left were empty, until Valerie sat down, just two seats away, an empty chair separating us.

The teacher entered, and after chatting briefly, closed his eyes and began meditating. After meditating for a time, he opened his eyes and meditated on each of us, one at a time. When he opened his eyes to meditate on each of us, he never gestured in any way, but remained deeply absorbed. The story I'm telling here is the only time I ever say him gesture in any way while meditating on anyone, especially in the dramatic way that occurred this evening.

Because Valerie and I were the last two people in the hall, far from the teacher, in the last row, it took some time for the teacher's gaze to come to me. I was sitting quite some distance from him, but that did not in the least diminish the power of the meditation. At last he came to me, and as that Beautiful Light and Dissolution-Bliss began to overwhelm me, suddenly I noticed movement out of the corner of my eye, to my left. Valerie had changed positions in her chair, hugging her legs to her chest, her feet resting on the chair seat, rocking from side to side. Lord help me! I brought my attention back to the teacher, who was still gazing at me, and thought, "Well this is just great. How typical. It seems every time you meditate on me these days, I'm thinking worldly thoughts. And now this."

To my astonishment, he made a sudden and exaggerated expression of puzzlement. What? Had he heard me? I dismissed it. But he kept that expression, his head actually tilted as if to ask me, "What are you talking about?" He had said that during meditation, he saw into our inner Being; a notion I'd generally dismissed as myth. Without expecting a response, I simply questioned within myself, "Is he saying that this spiritual affair has nothing to do with that

Mystical Experiences with My First Teacher

(carnal thoughts and such)?" He immediately raised his eyebrows up and down, exaggeratedly, like Groucho Marx, and nodded exaggeratedly. Others in the hall, like myself, must have wondered what on earth he was doing. Again I asked, inwardly, "It's got nothing to do with that?" and again, to my astonished amazement, he nodded affirmatively in the same exaggerated manner. He could hear me!? Twice he had responded immediately, in that exaggerated manner, to my inner musings. But… he never moved during meditation. What was happening. Valerie, to my left, was the last person in the hall, and his gaze moved on to her.

When this teacher would finish his open-eyed meditations on everyone, he would close his eyes and return to deep Immersion for a time, before opening them again. Even then, he did not speak immediately, but sat quietly, still absorbed, as were all present. But this time, the moment he opened his eyes, he turned, lifting his head slightly to look at me in the back of the hall and said, "We had a nice dialog."

The Little Lama

I did some line drawings for a book by my first teacher. One of them was of a small child who was a Tibetan Lama. Since I'd contributed to the book, I was among those asked to hand them out to fellow students. I noticed two women standing together in the line in front of me, each already holding a copy of the book. They must have gotten their copies from one of the others who were handing out books. I couldn't understand why they would be standing in my line. They seemed very excited about something or other. When it

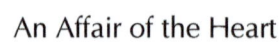 An Affair of the Heart

was their turn, they ran forward, wide-eyed and anxious to speak. They both had their books open to the page with the little lama, and almost simultaneously blurted out,. "Did you draw this?!" They went on to tell me that two weeks before – having not yet seen the picture – they had been meditating with the teacher in the desert and had both Experienced a vision of the little lama, only 200 feet high; a vision that they had verified to each other.

I didn't know what to say.

The Gazing

Once I sat crammed into the back seat of a small Honda with two other friends. Five of us were on our way to see my first teacher. He had called a special meeting for ten or so of the men who "studied" with him (I've never liked that word). On the way, the driver played a cassette of his favorite musician.

One song in particular touched me so deeply, as I associated it with this teacher. It impacted me with such an uncommon intensity that I had to turn my face to the window so no one would see the tears I could not hold back. I was awash in such deep gratitude for having found him, and the deep affection I held for him at the time.

Entering the house where the meeting was taking place, I was still awash, watery-eyed. The men attending sat in a semi-circle and the teacher walked into the room and sat close in the semi-circle. As he began talking he looked at me, and throughout the entire meeting, as he spoke on various things, changing subjects, he never looked away. Others had to have wondered what was going on. I simply lost myself in his gaze, his return of unspoken affection, and the

Mystical Experiences with My First Teacher

Dissolution and Bliss that always accompanied his presence, and most powerfully, that gaze.

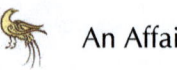 # An Affair of the Heart

The Onset of Existential Reality

Here in the world,
Most of us must work to survive.

During the period of spiritual Madness, the practical matters of existence were annoying considerations for which I had little time or interest. The mind only wanted to Immerse itself in Dissolution[45], and the Heart wanted only to Immerse itself in the Ecstasy that had Inhabited it, and was inherent in that Dissolution. But inevitably, livelihood became a pressing matter, and I was forced to face the stark facts of existence in 20th century America.

The great spiritualization of my life coincided synchronistically with the end of my musical career. Times had changed, and after the last long-term engagement, I found myself in a world where it was no longer possible to find steady engagements; and the engagements that could be found were at dingy bars, not fit to be called nightclubs. But even before all that was to happen to me, spiritually, life as a musician had lost its allure. I'd been fortunate, carried along by the cultural revolution of the '60s that had wound down by the late

---

[45] While simultaneously and confoundingly being obsessed with understanding what had happened, and what it all meant.

An Affair of the Heart

'70s. But that wave had washed me onto the shores of the '80s, and a far different cultural and existential reality.

The Horror

And so, although possessed by a terrible fear about my future, one by one, I began selling my musical equipment to get by until I could figure out a new way of making a living; a "figuring out" that seemed impossible, given my state of spiritual Madness, and the fact that after a lifetime as a self-taught musician, I had no marketable skills. If the fear that overwhelmed my every waking hour had not been accompanied by The Inner Radiance and the ongoing experiences with my first teacher, I don't know how I would have gotten through this period intact.

But as has always been the case in my life, friendships were a blessing. During this period, I shared this existential condominium with several others who were in relationship with my first teacher. One friend in particular was in the same transitional existential crisis that I was in. Having lived a simple but happy existence, he, too, found the foundations of that simple existence suddenly demolished, quite literally. As fate would have it, we both ended up sharing an apartment with a couple other students, all of whom were in the same existential boat. Passing each other in the hallway, we would mimic a line from the movie *Apocalypse Now*, whispering in growling, ominous tones, "The Horror." We joked, but the situation was truly horrifying.

Another comfort in this difficult time was my awareness that if worse came to worse, my beloved friend Michael's home would offer sanctuary where I could throw down a sleeping bag on his

The Onset of Existential Reality

living room floor and take refuge for a time, until I sorted out my life. He had saved me several times in my life as a musician, in the dry spells between bands and engagements.

But far more impactful on my state of being, the gut-wrenching fear I lived with was accompanied in each instant by the Inexpressible Fullness, Completion, and Bliss of The Inner Radiance; a Radiance that was untouched, unmoved, and impenetrable by the vicissitudes of outer circumstance and ever changing psychological states. When Attention dissolved into The Inner Radiance, the manifest world, the felt sense of my individuated self, and all of the troubles of manifest existence began to Dissolve into the Rapturous Experience of Timeless, Spaceless, Singularity.

And so there was a period that followed Divine Madness, in which the imperative of earning a living pressed increasingly upon my moment-to-moment awareness, coexisting with The Inner Radiance.

Learn to Type, and Have Faith

Selling my musical equipment meant I couldn't go back to life as a musician, as I had no money to replace the amplifiers, speakers, or keyboards. Selling off this equipment was traumatizing, and I spoke with my first teacher about my tenuous situation. To my surprise, without hesitation, he said, "Learn to type, and have faith." Unable to hide my skepticism, I blurted out, "Have faith?" I had long since lost faith, which had not been resuscitated in spite of all that had so recently happened to me, spiritually. Hearing my doubt, his expression changed to one resembling a small child whose feelings had been hurt, and he responded, apparently astonished at my skepticism, "Faith is what we're all about!"

An Affair of the Heart

And so, although lacking faith, I did in fact learn to type, and properly so, unlike the self-taught way in which I'd learned to play music. It seemed a fruitless effort, but I persevered fitfully, without much discipline. The true auspiciousness of his suggestion that I learn to type would only become evident within the months that followed.

At one point my money finally ran out and there was no more equipment left to sell. I put my last few dollars into gas, so I could drive south to San Diego and fall, once again, on the mercy of my old friend Michael. A pocket of change was my remaining personal fortune.

Salvation

A day or so before I was ready to leave, some friends who were also in relationship with my first teacher told me the company they worked for was looking for a secretary, and that it couldn't hurt to interview. I set up an interview, drove to the Century City high-rise where the office was located, put what I remember to be my last quarter in the parking meter, took the elevator to the 29th floor, interviewed, and got the job.

It was only a week or so, however, before I was fired. It was obvious to everyone involved that typing aside, I knew nothing of being a secretary. I was given the option, though, of moving to the basement of the building and becoming the shipping clerk for the company; a job that basically involved packing up and shipping computers. I took it, and was grateful to have it. I could remain in Los Angeles and continue seeing my teacher and the many friends I'd made in that community.

The Onset of Existential Reality

The Moment of Grace

Each day at lunch I would take the elevator up to the office and using one of the computers, type my spiritual journal. One day the Vice President of engineering, no longer able to tolerate the behavior of his partner in the business, walked into the engineering room, and walked out with two of the better programmers, the very friends who'd gotten me the job. He was leaving the firm, and starting his own company, and had invited the two of them to join him. As they were walking toward the door he paused as he passed me, typing away at my journal. He turned and said, "So Charles, do you want to be a technical writer? You type really well. Way more money." I said, "Yes."

Learn to type, and have faith. Perhaps the teacher's recommendation, my hobbled implementation, and the resulting fruition was all simply serendipitous coincidence? The whole affair is one of those things that occur in many of our lives, on the frontier of the miraculous, and each of us makes of it what we will. Whether miracle or happenstance, I had stumbled upon a means of subsisting in the world. Still… I had no faith.

Illumination in the Workaday World

There's no denying that working eight hours a day, five days a week, had an impact on my Divine Madness. The Inner Radiance did not diminish, but remained a constant; untouched, unmoved, impenetrable, as always, by the vicissitudes of outer activity or circumstance. But there was no escaping the fact that unlike the recent period of my spiritual idyll and unlike those living in an ashram, so much less time was now able to be given to contemplation

 An Affair of the Heart

and consideration, my Attention being focused, by necessity, on the workaday tasks at hand, 40 hours a week.

And yet, during moments of pause, when the acute focus of Attention would relax, The Inner Radiance would become evident, and often Brighten. Even during periods of intense outer focus, if I checked within, I would find that soft ambient Radiance, ever available to the return of Attention. There were also times when, unsolicited, The Inner Radiance would well up spontaneously, closing my eyes and taking my breath away for no apparent reason, dissolving awareness of the world and myself, of experience and experiencer. It also intensified in moments of extreme joy and sorrow, peace and panic. Again and again I was shown the immutable nature of The Inner Radiance. The conditions and circumstances of the "outer peripheral" world gave rise to reactivity in the "inner peripheral" world of psychology and emotion, but that ever-changing weather never touched, much less diminished, the moment-to-moment Experience of the Inner Radiance.

Disillusionment and Confusion

Nothing, it seemed,
Meant what I had hoped it might mean.

The Shattering of Naïve Expectations

After having read books on spirituality and enlightenment for those many years before meeting my first teacher, he was the first purportedly enlightened person I had ever met in the flesh. The friend who recommended him said he was enlightened. His students said he was enlightened. And he didn't hesitate to state, himself, that he was "fully Self-realized". But what they all meant by "enlightened" or "realized" was unclear to me, for in my time with him, he never proffered a clear, concise definition; only vague allusions that left me wondering.

I entered that first relationship with my own idealized notions about enlightenment and the qualities of an enlightened Being; the archetype of Jesus that I'd continued to hold to from my youth; a being who was utterly selfless, the "lesser" aspects of human nature having been subsumed by Love; a being full and complete within, free of all inner lack, with the sole agenda of Blessing all of creation. And early on in the relationship with my first teacher, my innate

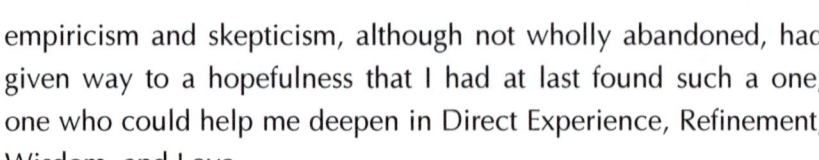 An Affair of the Heart

empiricism and skepticism, although not wholly abandoned, had given way to a hopefulness that I had at last found such a one; one who could help me deepen in Direct Experience, Refinement, Wisdom, and Love.

In hindsight, my expectations seem childlike and naive. But I have compassion for my younger self, for at that time, swept up in utter amazement at all that I was experiencing, and illumined with aspiration, not to mention the ongoing experience of The Inner Radiance, I did not see then, all that would become clear over time. Before meeting my first teacher, I had never had a spiritual experience of any kind, and was simply overwhelmed by the reality of so many experiences I would previously have dismissed as religious fantasy. And it had seemed to me, early on in the relationship, that my first teacher might well have been someone that embodied the archetype I held; his powers bent only on awakening and enlivening my Essence, inwardly, and opening my eyes, outwardly, to the Mystical nature of manifest creation.

After all, it was after the first meditation with this teacher that I'd experienced three days of a state of being in which the pain of selfhood, and other impossible-to-define aspects of inner pain, were vanquished, nowhere to be found. And it was only days later, after that liberated awareness faded, that I was driven by despair to the SRF gardens, where with fierce will and determination I had followed a path of inner enquiry to the Ecstasy-Without-Opposite of Nonexistent Existence, the Rapturous Essence of my Being. And it was in meditations with this teacher that I had experienced the powerful, Exquisite emanation of spiritual energy, the Inexpressibly Beautiful Light, our nonverbal dialogs, and so many other mystical experiences, including the confounding but life altering Vision of Lakshmi and Vishnu.

Disillusionment and Confusion

Cracks

I was only with my first teacher for two or so years, and it may have been as early as the end of the first year that I began to notice and become uncomfortable with certain of his statements and behaviors. These seemed antithetical to the attributes I associated with enlightenment and the enlightened, but those lofty expectations aside, they were troubling even at the most basic human level.

I saw what had seemed initially to be a confident self-assurance on the part of the teacher devolve into a painful-to-watch narcissism of increasing depth and breadth, until it seemed to have become pathological. It seemed to me – and yet again, this is not a statement of "truth", but only my perspective – that lingering residues of egoity had been resuscitated, and came to life with a terrible vengeance. His position as "an enlightened one" only seemed to facilitate an unrestrained passion for power and all that it entails.

The man who emanated that Beautiful Light and spontaneously "meditated" those in proximity became, more and more so, a caricature of one possessed by narcissism and greed. The nature of the teaching changed dramatically, as well, in conjunction with the increasing narcissism and troubling behaviors, in ways with which I had less and less affinity.

The dream of a "perfected" being alive in this modern era, it seemed, had been dashed. And having seen the human tendency to elevate and exalt, making more than should be made of those deemed holy, I wondered at the perfection of past saints, as well, of whom we only heard through the writings of their students or admirers. My faith in a living Christ-like being had been tenuous at best, even as I had allowed myself, briefly, desperately, to hope. But in the face of

An Affair of the Heart

this turning tide, in place of that tentative faith, a tsunami of doubt, confusion, and at times, despair, swept through me.

The End

Early in our relationship, my first teacher had taken me aside and told me he wanted me to teach, eventually. As preparation, he asked me to learn yoga. His plan was to have me lead yoga classes, and in that way introduce prospective students to his teaching. But whether through profound laziness, or because of the conflicts I was experiencing with his behaviors, I never followed through. I'm willing, in hindsight, to ascribe this failure most fundamentally to profound laziness. But things had also reached a point where I had no desire to propagate his teachings. In any case, my failure to learn and teach yoga was the cause for the end of our time together. After admonishing me time and again, he asked me, in a kind and loving way, to move on.

Leaving the many dear friends I'd made in the community was difficult; leaving the teachings with which I'd come to such a disconnect, was not. As for the teacher, himself, I remained torn and confused. If a dear friend becomes addicted in some way or other, you do not curse them, but try, as you're able, to help them. I left my first teacher not cursing him, but praying for him, with gratitude for the Blessing he had been in my life. And one of the greatest Blessings and Teachings I'd received was that spiritual power, whatever it may be called in the various traditions, however dazzling and miraculous in many ways, was not indicative of refinement across the whole of a being.

All of these things aside, while not excusing his behaviors, I remain

Disillusionment and Confusion

so very deeply grateful for having met this man. It's a confounding affair, and not simply a matter of black and white.

Encounters After

In the months after I left the community, I met the teacher on a couple of occasions; occasions on which he exhibited kindness and affection toward me, confounding me even further. For an aspect of his teaching was that after you were no longer with him, you would notice a diminishment in your spiritual energy. He also urged his students not to socialize with former students. These were, of course, very cult-like admonitions, and two among many other aspects of my estrangement from his teachings.

I'll Always Help You

In the first meeting I was at a restaurant with Ken, the friend who had seen the Vision with me, and who was still studying with the teacher. Being a true friend, and just a good person all 'round, he had ignored the teacher's admonition to avoid former students. To our surprise, the teacher entered with a few students, and they took a booth some distance from us. At one point, the students got up suddenly and found seats elsewhere. The teacher motioned to me to come sit with him. Deeply confused, I went and sat across from him. He asked how I was doing, and I responded, touching my chest, "It hasn't gone away." He asked what it was that hadn't gone away, and I replied, "The Inner Radiance." He said that it would never go away, and asked me why that was. I responded with the truth of my direct experience, "Because it's what we *Are*; it's our own Essence." He asked, "And why else?" I was disheartened by that question, and knew what he wanted to hear. I said, more as a question than a statement, "Because you're still helping me?" He nodded, and said, "I will always help you. Sometimes we love certain people more than others. We don't know why. Maybe it's because we see more of Eternity in them. You just need to be worn by the world a little more."

Worn by the world? More? My heart sank.

Get Down Here!

The second meeting was at a movie theater. Again, I was sitting with Ken, waiting for the previews to begin. We were in the middle of the theatre, by the left aisle. To our surprise the teacher walked down the right aisle with a few students, and sat several rows in front of us. At some point one of the students turned for some reason or other, and noticed us. He passed the word down the line of students to the teacher, who turned and waved as if to say, "Come sit with us." Remembering this teacher's statements that current students should not associate with former students, I sent Ken off, not wanting to keep him from proximity to his teacher. But after Ken joined them, the teacher, seeing this, turned with a look of exasperation, and gestured even more emphatically to me. As I joined them, sitting next to the student furthest from the teacher, the teacher leaned forward, turning toward me, and said, "Get down here, you idiot!"

Wandering the Wilderness

You just need to be worn by the world a bit more.
-My first teacher

Into the Wilderness

After the time with my first teacher ended, sometime around 1983, I wandered the spiritual wilderness for 20 years before the next significant event of my spiritual life. Twenty years is a long time, and of course much happened during that period.

On the domestic front I advanced in my career, establishing myself, at last, in a stable livelihood, moving ever upward in position and pay. I got married, purchased a home, and in short order transformed from an itinerant musician to a middle-class American, with all of its attendant benefits and deficits. But of course, after all that had happened, and with The Inner Radiance inhabiting my Heart, my seemingly normal life would never again be normal.

Spiritually, after the collapse of naive assumptions about enlightenment and the enlightened, these decades saw the deepening of confusion and disenchantment, and an ever growing cynicism about the whole spiritual affair – this in spite of all that

 An Affair of the Heart

had happened, and the Presence of The Inner Radiance. For year after year, teacher after "enlightened[46]" teacher was exposed in scandal after scandal, ranging in nature from revelations of mere human frailty to behaviors that were nothing short of pathological. Especially troubling was the fact that the majority of these scandals seemed to occur within the traditions involving the emanation of spiritual energy. These troubled me specifically because this had been the nature of my first teacher's path, the path on which all of the miraculous events of the past few years had come about.

Teachers in emanation traditions seemed more readily susceptible to succumbing to narcissism and its attendant ills. A contributing factor, no doubt, was the way students in those traditions, amazed at the emanation of spiritual energy from the teacher, and astounded by their own subsequent experiences, elevated those teachers in ways not common in other traditions.

The presence of spiritual powers[47] in a teacher only contributed further to this elevation, and in some cases deification. Certain among these traditions even institutionalized a worshipful relationship with the teacher.

A spiritual friend often joked that Los Angeles was "the Benares of the Western World" because teachers of almost any tradition who had attained some degree of celebrity would inevitably end up coming through LA, giving talks or meditations. During these 20 years of wilderness wandering, friends would call, asking if I had seen the latest teacher du jour, exclaiming how powerful their emanation was. This was invariably met with a disdainful dismissal

---

[46] Over time, the word "enlightenment" would become such a confused muddle that it lost all meaning or relevance.
[47] Such as the telepathy I experienced with my first teacher.

Wandering the Wilderness

from me; "Spiritual energy? Big deal, so what." The most embittered responses were reserved for those friends who equated powerful emanation with the attainment of enlightenment.

Most of the time throughout these years I succeeded in keeping despair at bay. But there were periods when it overwhelmed me, and I felt lost, isolated, alone, and desolate. A few friends from my first teachers community continued to stay in touch with me, and visit occasionally, in spite of his admonitions to the contrary. But those few oases aside, I wandered alone all those years, in a spiritual desert.

The Egoic War

It is always a danger to the aspirant on the path,
When one begins to believe and act as if the ten thousand idiots,
Who so long ruled and lived inside, have all packed their bags,
And skipped town or died.
-Hafez

If there was a hallmark of ongoing spirituality within me during these decades, it was the enduring struggle with the painful felt sense of my personal self, an egoic contraction felt across the whole of my manifest Being[48].

After the Experience of Nonexistent Existence and the advent of The Inner Radiance, I never for a moment considered myself enlightened, awakened, or any such lofty notion. For however Transmuting the Death-Unto-Life of Nonexistent Existence had been, and however Illumined with The Inner Radiance my ongoing

---
[48] See the chapter "On Having Become Someone".

 An Affair of the Heart

experience continued to be, I also continued to experience this contraction.

With each passing year, I became more deeply and desperately engaged in fruitless[49] and devastating warfare with that self; warfare that had begun the moment "I", the egoic self, had reappeared from the Heaven of Nonexistent Existence. As time passed I became more and more frustrated, for I had assumed that the presence of The Inner Radiance would, over time, dissolve the salt doll of egoic contraction. But the opposite seemed to be true, for the egoic contraction only increased in intensity as the years passed, becoming ever more unbearable.

It was a confounding scenario. For in my deepest interiority The Inner Radiance Shone untouched, unmoved, and impenetrable by this contraction. But in the peripheral aspects of my manifest being – the subtle energetic, psychological, emotional, and physical – the contraction remained. While all of my friends were of course aware of their own egoic contractions, for most it was not the increasingly painful and desperate affair I was experiencing. Many years later I would come to see that the increasing, rather than diminishing painfulness of the egoic contraction was, in fact, an aspect of its Dissolution.

Teachers During The Wandering

During those 20 years, in spite of growing cynicism, curiosity and a desire to find answers to lingering spiritual questions led me to see a few teachers, spending some time with two in particular who

---

[49] I can't be certain that this warfare was fruitless. But it seemed so at the time.

Wandering the Wilderness

played significant roles. And there was a man who, although not technically a teacher, would play a profound role in my life[50]. I saw a few others, as well, who did not influence me heavily, but none the less enticed and inspired me, and helped keep curiosity alive, each in their own way.

---

[50] See the chapter "Baba".

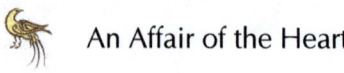 An Affair of the Heart

The Second Teacher of Significance

It's in the instant before the Upsurge.
-My second teacher

My Pundit Friend Comes Through

I call the teacher I'm about to describe "my second teacher" because he was the second teacher that had a profound impact on me, spiritually. I didn't "study" with him, because he had no such relationships. He only gave satsangs every once in a while, in which he would meditate briefly, give a brief talk, and then allow questions to be asked. Like my first teacher, there was little opportunity outside of this format to engage in a deeper spiritual relationship. That's not to say that he, like all teachers, didn't have closer friends among his students. But I, alas, was not one of those. Until his death I saw him whenever I could.

During the time with my first teacher, I made lifelong friends among the students. One friend in particular within that community had proven to be very helpful as a teacher in the academic sense. He had a high-level knowledge of various religious and philosophical

An Affair of the Heart

traditions which, although not necessarily deep, was broad enough to be deeply helpful to me. Although all that I learned from him did not put to rest my mind's confoundment, it helped me find a broader context within existing traditions and philosophies for all that had happened to me.

Among the traditions my pundit friend introduced me to was the Hindu philosophy of advaita vedanta. In that tradition I found described, to my amazement, the path of inward enquiry I had followed that day in 1981 at the SRF gardens. It was a remarkable revelation to find the intuitive way that I had followed described, more or less, in an ancient tradition. While the type of enquiry advaita prescribed was remarkably similar to my own, there were aspects which had not been part of my enquiry, and certain tenets with which I was not wholly resonant. This wasn't a concern, because I'd come to expect concurrent resonance and dissonance in my encounters with various traditions.

The very week the association with my first teacher ended, my friend – who, like a few other friends, refused to obey the teacher's injunction against fraternizing with former students – told me that the author of my favorite book on advaita was having a satsang that upcoming weekend. The timing was remarkable. And since advaita was the tradition with which my pundit friend had the most intellectual affinity, we both resolved to go see this teacher.

This would be my first time seeing an advaita teacher, and my friend stressed that there would likely be none of the mystical experiences I'd had with my first teacher, and no discussion of such things. There would almost certainly be no talk of Bliss, and I should forget about the Ecstasy of Nonexistent Existence (which this teacher had once deemed "a mere sweet", and a dangerous one at that). My

The Second Teacher of Significance

friend warned that with these things being so much a part of my experience, I might find the advaitic teaching and the nature of the satsang somewhat dry and intellectual.

The Fateful Meeting

The much anticipated weekend arrived, and I found a seat at the satsang. As I waited for the teacher to arrive, I noted that The Inner Radiance was welling up with uncommon intensity. This had always been the case with my first teacher, as well. But given my friend's admonitions, I was puzzled by its arising here.

The teacher finally arrived; a small, older, somewhat frail man. He sat in silence for quite some time. And as I sat there, I was swept away in a veritable tsunami of Dissolution and Ecstasy. I couldn't think, I couldn't move; I was in Rapture. Dualistic perception Dissolved and Attention was subsumed by the powerful Gravity of The Inner Radiance. I felt my Heart would explode in Ecstasy. And because I kept my eyes open as we sat there – I'd become accustomed to meditating this way with my first teacher – everything in my field of vision vanished completely in that Exquisite Illumination that I had, by then, become very familiar with. Mind and cognition Dissolved into Ecstasy, too Intoxicated to function. I could see only one thing in this field of Light in which everything else had Dissolved: the teacher, sitting in Silence, in that ultra-pristine clarity I called 6D. But all around him, nothing but blinding Luminous Radiance. This was completely contrary to what my friend had told me to expect.

Eventually, the teacher spoke briefly about advaita, then asked for questions. After listening to a few questions and answers that I did, indeed, find heady, tedious, and dry, I could no longer contain the

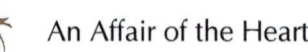 An Affair of the Heart

frustration that was, for me, at the heart of my spiritual life. I raised my hand and was recognized by the teacher. Expressing frustration and despair, not intending to be rude or hostile, but unable to restrain myself, I said, "So, we're just supposed to inquire in this manner, and keep inquiring, and keep inquiring, and keep inquiring, and keep inquiring, and keep inquiring, until one day, maybe, maybe – but don't count on it, because only a handful ever attain the goal – maybe one day Grace will fall on us?!" My bitterness may have been inappropriate, but I felt justified in my frustration, and oddly purged by having stated it openly.

He sat for a moment... and then, turning to face me more directly, leaned quite forward in his chair, and held his right arm out, low by his knees. He then brought his arm up quickly, in a shot, saying as he did so, "It's in the instant before the upsurge!" He held his arm in that higher position for some time, looking directly at me, and then, lowering his hand, he sat back slowly, saying, "In time, the Lover and the Beloved will become one." And then, leaning forward again and pointing at me, he said, as he jabbed his finger forward for emphasis, "Count on it!"

The instant before the upsurge clearly referred to what I was then calling Remembering; the Relaxing of Attention from outward fascination, back, behind, before, into the Essence of my Being, and the welling up, inherent in that Remembrance, of the Dissolution of dualistic awareness and The Inner Radiance, inherent in that Dissolution.

But... the upsurge? The upsurge?! How did he know about Remembrance and the welling up, the upsurge, of The Inner Radiance?! This was an advaitan, not a siddhi-imbued Mystic. How could he know?! We'd never met before. And according to my

The Second Teacher of Significance

pundit friend, advaitans didn't talk about "the upsurge" or other such experiential things. But this man knew, having never before met me?!

I left that satsang utterly perplexed. How did he know? How could he know? In the years in which I saw him after this first encounter, he never again mentioned such things, and adhered to the advaitic stance that my pundit friend had described.

I would go on to see this teacher whenever he offered satsang. But in fairly short order, I found myself uneasy with the particular advaitic stance that he taught, not resonant with many of its assertions. But I continued to see this teacher in spite of his teaching, because of the Mystical Alchemy of our relationship; because of that most Beautiful Light, and the fact that The Inner Radiance welled up powerfully in Affinity with this man, philosophical differences aside.

I saw him because of the direct experience of that which was otherwise simply being discussed in words; an experience in which the experiencer vanished, and the Ecstasy of Nonexistent Existence Flooded the experience of manifest existence.

Our relationship, outwardly, adhered to the advaitic protocol. I never mentioned The Inner Radiance, the Bliss inherent in Dissolution, or the translucent Radiance that filled the room throughout satsang with him. Mentioning such things would have brought a fatherly chiding.

He never once, in all those years, directly answered a question I would ask – a question that had arisen in the immediate context of the satsang. He always, instead, answered a more secret, private question that had been arising and persisting within me in the days

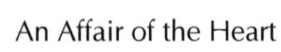 An Affair of the Heart

or weeks prior to seeing him; something I had not yet spoken of to anyone.

To this day I am confounded by the nature of our relationship, so contrary on the level of advaitic ideology, but so Magical on the level of The Inner Radiance that was Alive in me, Resonating with The Inner Radiance Alive in him.

Feeling Enquiry

Points of dissonance aside, there was one point with which I was in complete resonance with this teacher; he spoke often of *Feeling Enquiry*, as opposed to mere intellectual enquiry. The first time I heard this phrase from him, my Heart leapt, for this was what I had done that day at SRF, only a few years before meeting him. Having begun my inner enquiry with the mind, I found that it had soon reached the end of its utility, having led me through the process of identifying what I was not, and on to the realization that try as I might, I could not locate myself as an object, It was at that fateful juncture that I had turned to Feeling enquiry, for although I could not find myself as an object, I could, quite clearly, feel myself, the "I" feeling that I would later read that Ramana Maharshi, the advaitic saint, had spoken of.

This teacher also stated, often, that advaita and bhakti, mind and heart, were intimately entwined, inseparable, in any true enquiry. One without the other risked ending up in either dry intellectuality or sentimental emotionality. With this, as well, I was also in complete agreement, although I of course recognized that there are always exceptions to every rule.

The Second Teacher of Significance

A Sad Excuse

In the years I saw my teacher of advaita,
I went not to gain "understanding",
Or to follow, yet again,
The "nondual thread".

I went to bathe in the Radiance,
That emanated from that form,
Yes, my nondual friends,
From that form.

A shameless dualist?
Not so.

For somehow, impossibly,
Formlessness shone from that form,
And dissolved dualistic perception,
Including "me".

Before he even entered the room,
The world dissolved… "I" dissolved,
And all questions vanished.

A shameless "experience" junkie?
Not so.

For the experience,
Was of the experiencer vanishing,
Into That which was being discussed.

An Affair of the Heart

Discussed not in concepts,
Thoughts,
Words.

The words were a pretext.
The questions a pretext.
The answers a pretext…

For our simply sitting together…
Bathing in The Great Mystery,
That transcended the two of us,
And all duality.

Seeing him caused the Inner Radiance,
That had taken up residence in my Heart,
To Brighten like a Sun exploding.

Some Mystical aspect of our Relationship,
Dipped the salt doll of my "self",
Into the Ocean of Dissolution,
From which emerged, eventually…

Only a handful of Salt Water.

It did not happen through knowledge,
Or understanding,
Or seeing clearly,
Or a conclusion arrived at.

It happened through Grace.

The Second Teacher of Significance

The emanation of Formless Awareness,
In and as Manifest Experience,
Dissolving the contraction of self-identity,
In Satchitananda…

Existence, Consciousness, and Bliss.

Only in that Direct Experience,
Did I Understand all that I had heard,
In word, concept, and metaphor,
And knowledge became… Knowledge.

But make no mistake…

I went for the Light that filled the room,
In which my Entire Being Dissolved.

Shameless, I know.

I went for the Dissipation of mentation,
Into Serenity and Peace.

Shameful, I know.

I went for the Dissolution of Attention,
Into its Source.

How could I?!

An Affair of the Heart

I went for the Bliss of Pure Being,
Pouring into manifestation,
Overflowing the Wellspring of my Heart,
In relationship with that gentle, frail form.

Ponder this mystery, my nondual friends.
For this unfolded in physical proximity to,
In thoughtful remembrance of,
In heartfelt relationship with,
That gentle, frail form.

That's right… form.

For truly… truly,
Form is Formlessness,
Formlessness is Form.
Nirvana and samsara are One…

Those are not empty platitudes,
But the Living Teaching I received,
From Formlessness,
In and as that gentle, frail Form…

I'm a sad excuse for a nondualist.
How will I ever live this down?

Tough Crowd

*Come on, get out of the house,
Let's go see this teacher,
Everyone's on about.*
-My pundit friend

I was less than enthusiastic when, around 1991 or '92, friends in Los Angeles urged me to see a teacher who they said was much like my first teacher in the way of having powerful energy, and in certain aspects of his teaching. Both of these comparisons made my lip curl in disdain. How they thought such a teacher would interest me was simply beyond my understanding. But one day, supremely bored and simply wanting to get out of the house, I decided to go to a meditation being held by this teacher in Los Angeles. I arranged to go with the pundit friend who'd told me of my second teacher, and was eager, himself, to see this new teacher du jour. But I did wonder at the appropriateness of my attendance. After all, why bring a cynical attitude to a teacher's meditation. Why risk harming the aspirations of his students? Those considerations aside, I vowed to do my best to remain balanced.

We arrived at the meditation hall early, and I observed the students setting up the chairs, public address system, and otherwise helping

An Affair of the Heart

prepare the hall. Full of cynicism, forgetting my vow, I could not keep myself from curling my lip in disdain. Is this teacher for real, I wondered. Or is he, like so many others, a narcissist seeking power and all that accrues from it. I turned to look toward the back of the room, struggling to restrain the sour look on my face, and saw one of the students looking at me. Instantly aware of my bitter expression, I tried to quickly muster a smile. At the notion of harming another's aspirations, I felt a wave of bitter regret roll through me.

Eventually we sat down and the teacher walked to the front of the hall and sat on a chair placed there for him, elevated on a stage. Sarcasm aside, something about his face drew me, and without intending to, I liked him. Then it struck me with a shock; He was the person I'd seen looking at me, earlier, who I had taken to be a student!

During the meditation I saw the familiar Light, and felt myself, as I had with my first and second teachers, Dissolving into The Inner Radiance. After the first meditation the teacher turned to look directly at me, sitting a few rows into the audience, and said, "I see some of you have awakened kundalini. I salute you."

I didn't receive his salute well, inwardly, though I maintained outer decorum. I had always deeply disliked the term "kundalini", and the whole notion of its progressive, conditionally-based ascent through the subtle body. The Inner Radiance was not, in my mind, such a "thing" within the energetic body, but the Bliss of Hinduism's Atman, Sufism's Soul, my Essence, Shining into form.

A little perturbed, I thought to myself, "Why salute me? There's no attainment here, no merit involved!" No sooner had that thought completed than he continued, "It may seem to you that you've done

Tough Crowd

nothing to acquire this awakening, but I assure you, much, much effort was undertaken in previous lives." I was taken back. Was this another mind-reader?

He continued, still looking at me, "It's been a long time since we've encountered each other; since you saw me riding down upon you." Hearing that, I became extremely testy. I was so put off by the hierarchical nature of Guru Yoga as I'd experienced it that I couldn't restrain my inner irritation, and I thought, bitterly, "Oh yeah, right! It's always you, the great enlightened one, riding down on someone. How about *just once* it's you who is ridden down upon?" Still looking at me, his next sentence was accompanied by an expression of *his* being taken aback, "OK, maybe it was the other way around." Then, as if that wasn't enough to ensure I knew he could read my thoughts, he looked up and said to everyone, "Woah! Tough crowd tonight. A real check out scene!"

In the years that followed, I drove to Los Angeles now and then to see this teacher. Contrary to my initial expectations, he proved to be humble and kind. Each time I entered one of his meetings he greeted me at the door as a brother or friend, as happy to see me as I was to see him. Although not drawn to be in a spiritual relationship with him, I liked him, and that was reason enough for the drive.

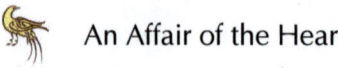 An Affair of the Heart

Baba

Slowly, slowly, Mother is doing everything.
-Baba

From June to December of 1996 I lived in Delhi, India. I'd been sent there on business, setting up a department for the company I worked for. When my manager informed our team that the company needed someone to volunteer to make this sojourn to India, in raising my hand I all but jumped out of my chair, and due to this unbridled enthusiasm, was given the assignment.

I arrived in India a spiritual basket case. In the years since the experiences with my first teacher, and in spite of the experiences with my second teacher, my spiritual confusion, depression, and cynicism had only worsened. It was during that time, not wanting anything to do with teachers or spirituality, yet still Illumined with The Inner Radiance, that I met the man I would come to call Baba.

Among its other meanings, the word "Baba" is used in India to refer to a father or a respected elder. The man I'm writing about resisted when I asked if I could call him Baba. "No, no. There is only

 An Affair of the Heart

Mother." He felt that even the commonly used term Baba elevated him too much.

I came to call him Baba because he was worthy of the word. He was, as you can tell from his reference to "Mother", a profoundly devotional Hindu. And yet, he was not bound in orthodoxy, and cared nothing for religious legalism.

My Friend Kaushik

I rested during my first day in India, recovering from a grueling series of flights that lasted twenty-some-odd hours. On the second day I was met at the hotel and accompanied to the office by Kaushik, the Administrator of the company's Delhi office. As we drove, we discussed my interest in India, and I mentioned my history of Hindu studies. When I mentioned Ramakrishna, Kaushik reached into his bag and took out a copy of *The Gospel of Ramakrishna*. He told me that in his youth he had attended school at the Ramakrishna mission in Kolkata.

Kaushik mentioned his "teacher" several times, but did not volunteer who it was. In my cynical state, I was in no mood to hear about, much less meet yet another teacher. But not wanting to be rude, I listened politely. Kaushik confused me, because while saying he had a teacher in one breath, he would then speak of the man as if he was merely a respected friend.

He said that his teacher-friend, a Mr. Roy, would be visiting him in November or December, and that I would surely get to meet him. He didn't tell me much about the man's spiritual state; whether he was enlightened, merely a psychic, or just a spiritual friend. But

Baba

the clear inference was that Mr. Roy was a man of some spiritual attainment who Kaushik deeply respected.

One evening, some months before Baba's visit to Delhi, I went to Kaushik's for dinner. Before dinner we sat on his balcony, overlooking a park, and talked about our spiritual lives. Restraining my bitter cynicism, I told him in a reasonable tone how I was not wanting or expecting anything spiritual to happen during my stay in India. He said that on the contrary, he was certain I would "get something." This was upsetting to me, as I had become so embittered of the notion of "getting" anything.

I had experienced so much, and had so many spiritual experiences, and none of it, including The Inner Radiance, had gotten rid of the painful contraction of egoic personhood that had become an ever-deepening torment in my life.

While we were eating dinner, he said, in a surreptitious tone, that he was not supposed to tell me about something, and that in fact it was a breach of spiritual protocol for him to do so. But nonetheless he went on to tell me that when he had first mentioned to Mr. Roy about the arrival of an American at work, Mr. Roy had said, after a dramatic pause, "He has come." That's the sort of dramatic pronouncement that's usually made by teachers when an intimate disciple shows up. And given my inner state, it made no sense to me, whatsoever. Certainly, when I had read such statements in various spiritual books, I had always hoped that one day I would hear those words myself, indicating that I'd found, at last, as Yogananda had, my nearest and dearest. But in my state of spiritual devastation, I was utterly unprepared to hear such words that evening. I simply didn't know what to make of it. I'd long since stopped thinking of myself as a spiritual seeker, in spite of all that had happened, much less a

An Affair of the Heart

seeker of any significance to anyone. If anything, spiritual bitterness had possessed me so deeply that I'd become the incarnation of bitterness and cynicism.

I Meet Mr. Roy

In November, Mr. Roy visited Kaushik's family for a week, staying at their home. As promised, Kaushik arranged for me to visit. Although skeptical of the whole affair, I was excited at the same time. It seems a tiny ember of hope remained hidden in my weary heart. Before the meeting, when I pressed Kaushik for more information on Baba, hoping to gain some insight on the etiquette I should observe, he told me that I should consider him a friend or older brother. There was absolutely no need for formality.

Kaushik still hadn't explained "what" this man was – a realized being, a psychic, still in bondage but highly advanced. He had spoken occasionally of having asked Baba questions about this or that, which led me to believe that at the least, he was someone whose counsel was valued. But if anything, that only made me a touch more skeptical.

When I arrived at Kaushik's, the living room was vacant, which was unusual. There was also little sense of activity in the adjoining kitchen. As we walked in, Baba entered the room, and Kaushik introduced me. I could see, just from these few seconds of interaction, that Kaushik was extremely respectful of Baba. No sooner had Baba and

Baba

I sat down, than Kaushik left the room, leaving us alone, and leaving me surprised, and feeling a little uncomfortable. I had thought we'd all be sitting and chatting casually.

Mr. Roy said that Kaushik had told him I might have some questions. I was stymied. I had no questions, and hadn't mentioned any to Kaushik. He seemed extremely serious, downright stern. I told him that I had no questions, but had simply hoped to chat with him.

Mr. Roy stated, straight out, that I was an elevated soul. This took me completely by surprise. I took it merely to mean that I was a spiritual seeker, for I was, in my view, far from elevated in any sense, spiritual or worldly. He went on to say that my "spiritual bloodline" began in ancient Kashmir. So… was he merely a psychic of some sort?

He said that I would return to America, then come again to India to finish some inner work that remained, then return to America to teach. Instantly everything became very, very far-fetched for me. Teach?! How could I possibly teach anyone anything. I was an absolute mess, psychologically and spiritually. He said I would be a peacemaker in an upcoming era of great turmoil and social unrest. It was impossible to believe. I was, after all, quite mad, and the antithesis of an "elevated" soul. When I protested, he said I would have no choice in the matter, that I had nothing to say about it, that I could not help but teach, that Mother was doing everything. The childhood dream of being a Mystic who could Bless flashed through my mind, but that glimmer of hope was quickly mocked by my self-loathing, as an absurdity.

I protested again, saying that I was crass and debased; if anything, a spiritual rogue along the lines of Girish Ghosh, Sri Ramakrishna's

 An Affair of the Heart

"bohemian" disciple, and that I couldn't possibly fulfill such a destiny. Girish was a playwright in Kolkata who was famous for serial drunkenness, womanizing, visiting brothels, cursing, and a longstanding addiction to opium[51]. I told Baba, with tears beginning to well up, that Girish, for me, represented the greatest hope for seekers on every path. For in spite of his nature he was transformed, transmuted, over time, by his relationship with Sri Ramakrishna, and the master's Unconditional Love.

I'd always marveled at Sri Ramakrishna's Unconditional Love for Girish, and how, against all spiritual orthodoxy, he'd simply left him to his ways, transmuting him from the inside out. Early on, Girish declared his disdain for spiritual disciplines and techniques, and, at any rate, his inability to adhere to them, even if he wanted to. Ramakrishna responded by asking Girish to give him his power of attorney, saying that he would accept full spiritual responsibility. It was that Grace that led Girish to become, as the more orthodox of Ramakrishna's disciples would declare, "Second to none," and "One of the jewels in Ramakrishna's crown." Girish ran contrary to all tradition and orthodoxy. When disciples spoke poorly of his behavior, Ramakrishna chided them, declaring that Girish was a seeker of the "heroic" type, that seekers of that type belonged in a class of their own, and his lifestyle would not harm him, spiritually.

When I read *The Gospel of Ramakrishna*, I took great hope from the story of Girish. For along with my intermittent (though extremely intense) spiritual aspiration came a deep well of samskaras, or conditionings, and a love of the Maya[52], the allure of manifest creation. My inner feelings had always been those of Girish. I held

---
[51] Girish used to say that the very ground upon which he sat was defiled; a statement that brought a quick rebuke and correction from Ramakrishna.
[52] The alluring manifest creation that some say entices attention away from God.

Baba

in disdain and contempt techniques and conditional achievements born of effort and merit. Love, Causeless and Unconditional, simply had to be the way. If it was not, I no longer wished to live in a creation that I would deem, in that case, to be a living hell.

After I'd explained how I perceived myself, and spoke of my affinity for Girish, Mr. Roy sat back, paused, then said matter-of-factly and with certitude and authority that I was in fact the modern incarnation of Girish Ghosh. Now my doubts were truly welling up, and I began to seriously doubt the voracity of this old man. I was already in complete shock at the things he had said, so this pronouncement was less stunning than it would otherwise have been. Still, I was numbed with bewilderment, and feeling ever more uncomfortable.

After I'd spent quite some time chatting with Mr. Roy – I wish I could remember all of the things he said – Kaushik returned to the room. When Mr. Roy mentioned that I was Girish, Kaushik joined me in laughing dismissively. What could we do? It was all too much. But Mr. Roy remained quite serious, and turned to Kaushik, saying chidingly, "I am telling you, he is the modern day incarnation of Girish Ghosh." Of course I didn't believe him, and don't have any idea to this day if he was seeing accurately. In any case, it doesn't matter, really.

I stayed for several hours, chatting with Mr. Roy and Kaushik. At one point it was time for Mr. Roy's morning puja. Kaushik's parents had a little closet beneath a staircase, much like the one Harry Potter lived in during his youth, converted to a worship area, replete with a little altar. Mr. Roy entered the little room, closed the door, and did his puja in solitude. After he emerged, we all sat around as he played the harmonium and sang a Love song to Divine Mother. I could see the tears in his eyes when he finished.

An Affair of the Heart

Who was this man?

A Second Meeting

The following day I returned to Kaushik's to speak again with Mr. Roy. The things he'd said in our first meeting were too crazy to believe, and in spite of having been put off somewhat, I was at the same time excited to speak with him further. He was simply a very pleasant fellow, and I couldn't help but like him. In spite of his initially stern manner, he was kind and humble, and clearly a Lover of his Divine Mother. This second meeting would prove almost as astounding as the first.

I began by saying, rhetorically, "I need to work on refinement, don't I?" He sat back and nodded kindly, but affirmatively. I have always felt "common," unrefined, and inelegant, especially in the spiritual sense. I was certainly no saint, and far from the "elevated being" he'd spoken of in our first meeting. But while I knew he was right about my needing refinement, seeing him nod in agreement hurt me deeply, none the less. My eyes began to tear up, and I struggled to hold back the floodgates and keep from breaking down altogether. I said, through sobs, "I will say this only once, and then will not mention it again." He seemed puzzled, and drew nearer. I said, "Sir, I'm so sorry for being so rough-edged. I apologize in advance for anything I might say or do in the future that might offend, seem to show a lack of respect, or in any way be unpleasant. I don't mean any harm." Then I could no longer hold back the tears.

Mr. Roy appeared shocked, and with an expression of deep concern, said that I mustn't say such things, that he was so happy to have met me, that I had done so much for him. What could I possibly have

Baba

done for him? "When I first saw you..." he hesitated, searching for words, then said, "Ask Mother what you have done for me?" He said that I had no idea what an elevated being I was. I would do such great things, I would help so many. I would have no choice in the matter. I would not be able to stop myself. Mother would do it all. He said that now Mother was playing with me, but one day I would play with Her[53].

I said that it all seemed impossible to me. I simply could not abide spiritual disciplines, much less the rigorous lifestyles that had been led by spiritual teachers I'd read about. He said, "You don't need to do that. You've already done all that."

You've read about my state of being prior to visiting Mr. Roy, about my years of lunacy and depression, about my abandonment of spiritual search. Mr. Roy's words seemed utterly impossible! I could not doubt what I knew to be my inner state, so I doubted, instead, Mr. Roy's ability to see, psychically. He was a very nice man who clearly had a good heart. But what else was he? Why was he telling me all these things, and with such incontrovertible certainty? How did he come to think all of these things? What was going on?

I told him that one could not teach what one did not know, and that words were a lesser teaching I had no interest in. True teaching was, I said, the ability to emanate Blessing directly. He said it would be so. I could not believe him. He said not to worry about my depression, that it was Mother playing with me, preparing me, somehow. It was spiritual. That, too, in the moment, didn't help me at all, and caused me to doubt him even more.

---

[53] Something he said often, but which I've never understood to this day.

 An Affair of the Heart

I told him how I often wished for a teacher, as I felt so crazy and isolated, spiritually. He said emphatically that I didn't need an outer teacher, that Mother was my teacher, with me always, and would teach me directly. Desperate for a different answer, I asked him again if I he was certain I would ever meet a guru. I subscribed to the notion that while there were many teachers in life, only one guru took us through the final steps. Relenting, he sighed and said yes, but added that I would spend only a very brief time with my guru, and that he would offer only a very few pointers, and then not linger with me[54]. To me it seemed such a solitary, lonely path that he described.

I also pestered him about whether there wasn't something I should be doing, spiritually. Again, he resisted saying anything, but finally relented, saying that all I needed to do was spend a little time with Mother in the morning and evening, and of course whenever I felt like it. But when he said this, it seemed he was more interested in stopping my badgering than giving real guidance. There was no need for formality or ritual, he said, for candles or incense, or an altar; no need for a set time or duration.

He was, however, quite emphatic in saying that I was to let no one stand between me and these meditations. Alas, I was my own greatest obstacle in this regard.

In spite of the Vision I'd had of Vishnu and Lakshmi, I remained confused about the existence of God, Divine Mother, or the like, and wondered if The Inner Radiance was the Mother he was referring to. Because that Radiance was ever-available, I suppose you could say

---

[54] Being dense, it took me many years to realize that among all of the people of importance to me, including Baba, he was the only one I spent only a few days with, and I had to drag pointers out of him, as he was insistent on not telling me what to do.

Baba

that I was in continual relationship with Her, assuming, of course, that She was that Radiance. In any case, when I thought of Her The Inner Radiance welled up powerfully, as if responding to my Remembrance.

When we parted at this second meeting, he said we'd meet again in this life, and that we'd have more time together. I said, "I hope so," and he replied, smiling, "Hope has nothing to do with it!" Again, that certitude and authority. Once he had told Kaushik something or other, and Kaushik had asked, "Really?" Mr. Roy replied, "I have said so." There was no egotism in such remarks. He was emphatic that everything was Mother, and Her will. He refused any attempts to elevate him, personally, to a higher station. Whether he was delusional or not, he felt that his certitude was merely a reflection of Her assurances.

Mr. Roy Becomes Baba

After Mr. Roy returned to Kolkata, I decided to call him Baba. I did this not out of any hyped up reverence, but simply because I liked him, and thought of him as a father. When Kaushik told Mr. Roy in a phone conversation that I was calling him Baba, Mr. Roy said, "He's such a nut!" But in no time at all, both Kaushik and Subhra, his wife, were speaking of Baba instead of Mr. Roy.

Diwali

After Mr. Roy returned to Kolkata, I experienced the Diwali celebration in Delhi. On Diwali, there's a tradition of setting off firecrackers and fireworks. It's my favorite Hindu holiday, based in

An Affair of the Heart

large part on the experiences I'll describe here.

I spent the earlier part of Diwali evening alone in the flat. But the plan was that at 11:00 o'clock I would take a cab to Kaushik's, and we would go together to the Kali Puja at the main Kali mandir, from midnight till 3 a.m.

As I sat at home earlier that evening the crackers, as firecrackers are called in India, which had started going off randomly in the late afternoon, started to increase in frequency. I decided to sit in front of the little altar I'd set up in the living room of my flat, put on headphones, and listen to some inspirational music. But as I sat, my mind was frenetic, restless and scattered, and I was not at all in a mood to contemplate, meditate, or even listen to music. On the brink of getting up, the picture of Lakshmi on the altar caught my attention, and I noticed how Incredibly Beautiful She was. And as I sat gazing at Her, to my surprise, given my mood, in the same manner that had happened during the Vision, Her figure became luminous, attaining that sense of dimension beyond normal sight. And as She had during the Vision, Her expression changed, and changed, and changed again, and as She had during the Vision, She occasionally turned into Vishnu, covered in shimmering golden adornment.

I noticed, in a way I'd never done before, how Unimaginably Beautiful Lakshmi was. Her Beauty struck me so intensely that I burst instantly into tears, and I found myself awash in a Pure, Romantic Love that I'd never experience before in my life. The mere thought of Romantic Love for Lakshmi would previously have seemed wholly inappropriate to me, wrapped as it usually is in sexuality. But there was no sexuality in this Love; only the Purest Essence of Romantic Affection and Longing. I'd never known this

Baba

kind of feeling could exist, free of physicality, and at first I remained perplexed, not knowing what to make of it. But the feeling remained and intensified, and for the first time in my life, unimaginably, I was seeing Her as my Beloved, not my Mother. I looked upon Her Beautiful form, and felt myself awash in Pure Affection and Longing. She was the very embodiment of Beauty, and… I had the absolute certitude that She *knew* me. She was my very own Love. Some part of my heart burst forth that had never before found expression. I had no desires to ask from her. I only wanted to give to her. I heard the sounds of crackers bursting outside, even through the headphones, and with each blast, I felt an indescribable Power exploding within The Inner Radiance.

With each blast I said, "Jai[55], my Love! For you." I don't believe I have ever cried so deeply, though the stories on these pages are so full of tears.

I turned then to the picture of Mother Kali, and broke down yet again. "Mother!" I demanded, "Cut the knot[56]!" I repeated the demand like a mantra, over and over, each time with increasing intensity. I was desperate, impatient, and angry. I'd had enough. "Cut the knot!" I screamed, inwardly, again and again and again, between sobbing breaths. The Inner Radiance had taken on a Quality I'd never known, of Power, and Victory. I don't know how else to explain it.

I got up and walked onto the back veranda and beheld an amazing wonder of fireworks, and such Glorious sounds of bursting power all around. There's no describing the ceaseless frequency of the explosions. It was as if the city was under a relentless siege. There seemed no gap in the fireworks, as was my experience during 4th of

---
[55] Victory!
[56] The knot, the contraction, of embodied personhood, of separativity.

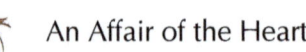 An Affair of the Heart

July celebrations in the States. There were continuous explosions of Glory, filling the skies over Delhi.

I was awash in a strange confluence of Pure Romantic Love and Unconquerable Power. Amazed at the incredible beauty of the fireworks, Pure Romantic Love overwhelmed me, and I said to Lakshmi, "For you. For you." Feeling the power of the explosions, seemingly everywhere around me, I cried to Kali, "Jai Ma! Jai!" Reading these paragraphs, my empirically-minded friends are no doubt nodding with certainty that I had gone quite mad, and most likely remain so.

I lit candles along the terrace wall, as is the custom, and brought Lakshmi's picture out. Then I ran back into the flat and brought out Mother Kali's picture as well. I raced into the house again, and brought out sweets to place in front of their pictures. I was, in these moments, quite the Hindu.

I stood on the veranda for perhaps an hour, tears flooding down my cheeks. "For you, Beautiful one!" "Jai! Jai!" "Cut the knot! Oh Mother, please, cut the knot!"

The bitter despair and cynicism that had become my ongoing condition regarding spirituality were, for a brief period, pushed aside by a powerful tide that was clearly not of my making. Perhaps Baba was right, and Mother – whatever that meant – was indeed doing everything.

With Baba in Kolkata

Kaushik and I arranged to visit Baba in Kolkata from December 6th through 8th. We stayed at Baba's house. My personal goal for the

Baba

journey was to see the Dakshineswar temple compound where Sri Ramakrishna had lived. I'd re-read *The Gospel of Ramakrishna* for the third time while in Delhi, and it had reminded me of my first love for Divine Mother. Now I would see the actual temple, and the master's room where so much of the gospel took place.

Friday was a day of relaxation, taking tea, and chatting with Baba. This day, and the remainder of my time visiting him, he would continue to tell me the same sorts of unbelievable things he'd spoken of in Delhi.

On Saturday we went to Dakshineswar. No sooner had we gotten into the car than I became deeply pensive and awash in emotions regarding Ramakrishna and the time in which he had lived. I was going to the actual temple he'd worshipped at, to the actual idol of Mother Kali, and to the very room in which he'd lived during the period described in the gospel. In my mind I saw scenes of him riding a carriage through the ancient streets of Kolkata, on his way to a play by Girish, and saw the familiar characters arriving at his room. It had been such a different world. A world in which spirituality and fellowship with all of those characters had been woven into my life. And now… here I was, stranded, alone, abandoned by the master, in what seemed in comparison, at that moment, a spiritually vacuous world.

I was sitting in the front seat with the driver, with Baba, Kaushik, and Subhra crammed in the back. He had insisted. About half-way to Dakshineswar I became overwhelmed with emotion, and had to turn my face as if looking out the window, so no one could see the tears I was struggling to hold back. Only fear of embarrassment kept me from bursting openly into sobs. Oh God, I missed Ramakrishna so. That time, and the players in that beautiful Lila. I did not have

 An Affair of the Heart

anything like a past-life vision, but had an overwhelming sense of having been there, and of mourning the passing of it all with a near-unbearable intensity. This uncommonly intense melancholy lasted the entire journey to Dakshineswar. It was fortunate that I was alone in the front seat with the driver. Nobody seemed to mind that I wasn't taking part in the back seat's lively conversations.

When we reached Dakshineswar Baba took me aside and walked with me into the Panchavati, the park next to the temple compound where so much of the gospel took place. The Ganges flowed close by. The whole compound was nestled right on the banks of the river. There was the tree under which Totapuri had taught Ramakrishna advaita, and under which the master had entered nirvikalpa samadhi.

Next we went to the Kali temple. Baba purchased the necessary offerings for us to give the priest when we made our way to the inner shrine. There was quite a queue, but in time I was standing in front of the very idol that had been the locus of so many of Ramakrishna's experiences. I was not prepared for the intensity of the experience. Although excited about seeing that inner sanctum, I'd expected nothing. I stood there, speechless.

Finally we came to Ramakrishna's room. I approached with Baba, who was in front of me, and entered. But as I approached the doorway, I could control myself no longer, and broke down, sobbing so deeply that I gasped for breath. I moved away from the door, trying to hide next to a window that looked into the room. I tried to suppress the emotions, feeling conspicuous so near the doorway. I saw Baba step back out when he'd noticed I'd not followed him into the room, but when he saw my state, he went back in.

Baba

When I regained enough composure, I stepped inside and took a seat on the floor, against a wall near the master's bed. All along the walls, near the ceiling, were pictures of all the disciples. There was Girish Ghosh. I did not want to close my eyes and meditate, again not wanting to be conspicuous. Meditation was not, for me, a public thing, and I felt awkward with so many people sitting around; none of them meditating. But Kaushik's little daughter, Kolyaani, who was just 5 years old, walked over to me from her position near the exit door, and chided me, saying, "Eyes closed!" I closed my eyes, and felt The Inner Radiance absorb me. But I soon became self-conscious, and opened my eyes. Again little Kolyaani saw me, and ran over, pushing my shoulder and chiding, "Eyes closed!" This must have happened two or three times. But each time, closing my eyes to appease her, I opened them again in short order, just too uneasy.

On Monday Baba would ask me if I'd seen any lights or anything as I was entering the master's room. It was an odd question from him, as so far in our brief interactions, he had never addressed that sort of thing. I told him I hadn't, and just let the question go. But later, curious, I asked him why he'd asked me that, and he said that as I had started to enter the room, he had turned back toward me, and saw Divine Mother touch me. This, he said, was why I had begun crying so uncontrollably and had to turn aside.

We left the master's room and wandered the grounds. I went down one of the two ghats, and stood with my feet in the Ganges. We then walked around the shops where there were beautiful pictures of Ramakrishna, Mother Kali, and all the Gods and Goddesses. I had my picture of Lakshmi at home; the one I'd meditated on at Diwali. "Mother! Cut the knot!" Kaushik purchased a couple of posters and had them framed for his parents at home. It was important to him

 An Affair of the Heart

that Baba hold them, then hand them back to him. This gesture made me feel that Kaushik did indeed see Baba as a holy man.

On the way home, we stopped at the home of a family that had requested a visit from Baba. There were some problems they wanted to discuss with him. Again I thought, "Who is this man, that others call on him this way?" When we arrived, one of the women took the dust of Baba's feet[57]. Kaushik told me Baba didn't like such attention, but laughed that she'd beaten him to the punch.

After we returned home we were taking tea and chatting, and I expressed, for the umpteenth time, disbelief at the things Baba was telling me. Frustrated, he said that when we'd stopped to visit the family on the return from Dakshineswar and he'd spoken with them privately, they'd voluntarily praised the spiritual state of the Westerner who was with him. "How did they know?" he asked. "I didn't tell them anything." This only made me cringe.

On the day we left Kolkata, Kaushik and I were in the room we'd shared during our stay. I was packing my bags when Baba came into the room. I took the opportunity to ask him formally if it was alright to call him Baba. "No, no," he responded firmly. "There is no Baba, no Charles. There is only Mother." I replied that yes, I had a Mother who was not visible to me – most of the time, at least – but needed a Father to talk to, here in this world." Kaushik fell backwards on the bed, laughing, saying, "Jai Charles!" Baba acceded.

---

[57] Touching the top of someone's feet in a gesture of respect.

Baba

Conversations With Baba After my Return to the U.S.

When I returned to the States, I called Baba every now and then, as much simply to say hello and hear his voice as to seek advice on this or that, because he was supremely reticent to give me any advice.

Regarding His Prophesies

Baba would sometimes make prophetic statements about mundane things that were going to happen in the short-term, and they didn't. I questioned him outright about these, and he said that in such matters, he spoke from what he saw in those moments, but such mundane, short-term circumstances can quickly change. I remained deeply skeptical. I confessed that his explanation aside, this made me feel doubtful and uncertain regarding the things he'd said would come to pass in my life. He became emphatic, insisting that all he had told me would come to pass. "It was true when I told you in India. It's true now, as we speak. And it will be true when I die. You have nothing to say about it. Slowly, slowly, Mother is doing everything."

To this day, I doubt all that he said – although thus far, it has indeed come about. And doubts about Baba and Divine Mother aside, to this day I am in relationship with this Divine Mother, who I address with many names, and clothe in many imaginal forms, knowing full well that She is none of them, and all of them; Nothing, and Everything; Formlessness, and form; Shiva, and Shakti.

 An Affair of the Heart

Regarding My Dreams

Several years after returning from India, I went through a period where I would awaken in the middle of the night, horrified, hyperventilating like a frightened rabbit, knowing with absolute certainty that I was dying of a terrible disease that would slowly and painfully take me down. The feeling was so real that even after sitting up in bed, it was not as happens with a dream, where you realized it was just a dream, and are immediately relieved. It took some time for the absolute certainty and its accompanying terror to subside. This, too, according to Baba, was Mother's work. He said I was experiencing this because in time, when I would meet people in such a condition, I would be able to relate from experience, and not simply what I'd read or heard.

My Fierce Loathing of the Divine Plan

Another time I called him, more frustrated than usual with notions I'd read in scripture of the "Divine Plan," in which suffering is said to be a means of our coming to perfection. I told him that if Divine Mother had indeed created such a plan, I was not on Her side, that I stood against Her, and would do so for all of eternity. "I realize I'm a meaningless speck of dust in the infinitude of creation," I said, testily, "But this speck of dust stands against such a Divine Plan." Taking what some would call blasphemy even further, I said, "Only the dark angel himself would devise such a cruel plan." Growing still more deeply upset I declared that if She was in fact responsible for this Divine Plan, She was the "Architect of Hell" and the "Mother of Sorrows".

Now you can imagine how an orthodox person would have responded to my blasphemous ranting. But Baba's response was in

Baba

a tone to match my own, "Yes! You tell Her to go to hell! You have every right to be upset! If She will not explain Herself, you tell Her to go to hell!" Then, after a long pause he assumed a gentle, loving tone, and said, "Just don't stop talking to Her."

Regarding Seeing Teachers

Occasionally I would find a teacher that fascinated me and would venture off to see them. Baba was always perplexed by this, and advised me not to go see teachers, stating that I was my own teacher; that Mother was my guru, directly. But my mind remained curious about certain aspects of spirituality, and I sought answers here and there. And I also enjoyed the time spent with the spiritual friends who accompanied me.

Regarding Self-Perfecting

I once mentioned to Baba that if I had one wish, it would be to be a more virtuous person. This was the only time he ever snapped at me. "That is none of your concern! You have nothing to do with that!" he chided.

I'm sure he didn't intend for me to abandon self-awareness and attention to the effects of my actions in the world. I feel he was addressing the endless and unproductive spiral of self-assessment, self-judgment, and as is so often the case, self-recrimination and condemnation that so many of us can become caught up in. But... I'm only guessing.

An Affair of the Heart

Regarding Scriptures

I mentioned to Baba that I enjoyed reading certain scriptures, but more often than not became disgruntled with the strictures and legalisms of orthodoxy. He surprised me by saying, "If you enjoy reading scriptures, by all means do so. But for God's sake, don't apply them to your life!"

Regarding The Inner Radiance

For many years I assumed The Inner Radiance was the same spiritual energy that emanated from the teachers I'd been drawn to. Those teachers had spoken of that energy as "shakti", and so, when chatting with Baba, I used that term. Naturally, I spoke of it often in my conversations with him. At one point he became a little disturbed, and said, "You're always talking about shakti. Why are you so obsessed with shakti?" This struck me as odd, because having assumed that what I would later refer to as The Inner Radiance was shakti, why would I not speak of it often, as the most Beautiful aspect of my ongoing experience? And I told him as much.

The phone connections to India were not the best, and it seemed that Baba sometimes did not understand, or misunderstood things that I'd said. So speaking very slowly, taking care to enunciate very clearly, I explained to him in great detail my experience of what I had been calling shakti; how it came about after samadhi – I did not then use the Sufi term of Nonexistent Existence – and had thereafter had its locus in my chest, in the area roughly around my heart; how it welled up when I read passages of spiritual books with which I was in resonance, or when I thought certain thoughts or the senses presented certain things; How it welled up with uncommon intensity when I meditated with others, and on, and on.

Baba

After a long silence, Baba said, "Oh Charles... that's not shakti. That's Ananda; the Bliss of the Atman." Hearing this, I explained the source of my confusion. He responded by saying that shakti is a particular spiritual energy, not to be confused with Ananda.

Shakti, he said, is an innately pure energy. But just like air or water, it can be a vehicle for pollutants. Many teachers, he said, are imbued with shakti, and the power to emanate it to others. And often, tragically, it carries the teacher's desire for power, or other polluting motivations and agendas still latent in their being. Also, although shakti may dazzle the recipient in a variety of ways, it does not, by itself, bring about Benediction, taking root in the aspirant's heart, and growing, thereafter. Certain seekers, of course, will benefit, regardless. But most often this is not the case.

Ananda, he said, emanates from the Heart of Being, and Blesses immediately and forever, even if the recipient notices nothing whatsoever in the way of spiritual experience.

Baba's Passing

As Baba grew older, into his 80s, he had more and more difficulty with his knees. And another illness of some kind was plaguing him more and more. But he didn't want to spend time talking about those things. At one point he said that he was losing his will to continue.

And then, quite near the end, he told me one day, "From this point forward you must trust your Heart, your intuition, *absolutely*, even if it tells you to kill someone." Of course he didn't mean that I should ever kill anyone, but only that this was the level of trust I must place

An Affair of the Heart

in my own sense of things from this point onward. I knew, then, that the end was near, and I was about to be on my own. Baba passed in 2013.

Other references to Baba come later in this book; things he said at certain junctures in my life, mentioned in the context of those times.

The Third Teacher of Significance

*No, please,
Spare me another "enlightened master".*

At the Turn of the Century

It would only be later in life that I would discover and feel a deep resonance with certain aspects of Sufism. And over the decades of Wilderness Wandering my interest in Buddhism had been sporadic and generally ambivalent. It's safe to say that after meeting my first teacher, until I delved more deeply into Sufism sometime in the 2010s, certain aspects of Hinduism were the broader context of my relationship with The Great Mystery. It was within that context that I met the last of the teachers who would have a significant impact on my spiritual life.

With this teacher there was none of the subtle-physical phenomena experienced with the other teachers I'd been in relationship with; no gold light or subtle-physical visions during meditations. In the end, the hallmark of my time with this teacher would be the experience of profound inner transmutations regarding the lingering contraction of personal identity. In relationship with my first teacher I had become

An Affair of the Heart

Illumined with The Inner Radiance. In relationship with this last of my teachers, I would come, at last, to Liberation from the terrible contraction of the personal selfhood that had plagued me for 20 years after the Experience of Nonexistent Existence. But I'm getting ahead of myself.

The Spiritual Stance I Had Arrived At

Since the dramatic experience of meeting my first teacher, I had never attributed the great transmutations of my spiritual life directly to any of my teachers. Although deeply grateful, respectful, and somewhat in awe, I was never worshipful, as so many on the emanation paths tend to be, and as those paths so often encourage. As I've said ad nauseam, I learned early on that the ability to emanate spiritual energy did *not* equate to a perfected being, or even negate the possibility of pathology. While I recognized the unique nature of every teacher's emanation – like the varied fragrances from different flowers – and their unique contributions to my spiritual evolution, I did not ascribe to the notion that they were directly responsible, mystically orchestrating our spiritual evolution.

As I see things to this day, our lives have a higher producer, script writer, and director, and we and all who we encounter during the play, are merely players on the stage. At the risk of redundancy:

> For the Teacher, one has gratitude,
> But love and devotion is for God.
> -Hazrat Inayat Khan

The Third Teacher of Significance

Oh God, Not Another One

It was September of 2001 when my pundit friend – the one I had met while with my first teacher, and who had introduced me to the writings of my second teacher – began talking about a teacher he was seeing; someone I'd never heard of, and in whom I had absolutely no interest. For I remained firmly established in bitter cynicism about the emanation paths and Guru Yoga, both of which, my friend told me, were aspects of this teacher's teaching. In fact, at this point in time I was exasperated with the entire external spiritual affair.

My friend's exclamations about how powerful this teacher's spiritual energy was only further put me off. Over so many years I had sat for so many hours in so many meditations with so many teachers who were powerful emanators of spiritual energy. All those times seeing all those teachers; all of that Light and power absorbed; all of those spiritual experiences; those countless moments of ecstasy and hope; so many tearful cries of hopelessness and despair; what good had all of it done? For in spite of the experience of Nonexistent Existence and the advent of The Inner Radiance, the pain of bondage to personal identity had only deepened excruciatingly over the years. Being Illumined with The Inner Radiance was undeniably an Unimaginable Grace, but I longed for Liberation, as well, from bondage to personhood.

As I'd expected, once I yielded to my friend's urgings and decided to see this teacher, a powerful tsunami of disenchantment, bitterness, and resistance welled up. Making matters so much worse, this teacher's web site declared him to be not only an "enlightened master", but an avatar, as well. You can imagine the lip-curling

 An Affair of the Heart

disdain that such declarations gave rise to within me[58]. What sort of person would make such claims, or more deceptively, allow others to do so on their behalf, so that they themselves might appear humble? Enlightenment? What was that? I had no idea what the word even meant anymore. It was certainly not, in my estimation, simply being imbued with spiritual energy, or the ability to emanate it. Nor was it profound intellectual apperception, arriving at an unshakeable conclusion, as was so common in contemporary nonduality.

My friend's suggestion came in the 18th year after the end of relationship with my first teacher. The Wilderness Wandering of twenty years was drawing to a close, although at the time I had no inkling of that being the case. On the contrary, this was a period when I was so deeply distraught that I mourned breathing in after breathing out; nearing the end of the most painful decades of my life.

In The Pit of Despair

I lost my job in May of 2001, not long after the technology bubble collapsed, and in the wake of that collapse, remained unemployed for a year and a half. That alone was stressful and frightening. But in addition, other aspects of my life had become unbearably painful, worthy of the phrase "soul crushing".

Once, in a phone call with Baba, I expressed the fear that having lived so long in such a psychologically painful state had brought me to a place where I was actually dying. He laughed, stating that I simply could not die until I had fulfilled Mother's work. He

---

[58] As they do to this day.

The Third Teacher of Significance

was emphatic that my death at that time was an impossibility. My affection for the man, however, did not translate into acceptance of what he said.

During another conversation with Baba I was so distraught I could barely keep my composure. To my surprise, I heard him struggling to suppress a chuckle. Then later, as I continued, finally bursting into tears, he again suppressed a chuckle that finally broke into gentle laughter. "I'm sorry," he said. "I'm sorry. I'm not laughing at you. I understand your pain is real. It's just that… I know something you don't." Taking on a more serious tone, he said that I couldn't skip these difficult chapters of my life, and was experiencing them so that in the future, when the brokenhearted came, I would speak to them from experience, not acquired theoretical knowledge or imagination. Making me terribly uneasy, as he had always done, he said I was not born for myself, but for humankind. Yet again, my affection for the man did not translate into acceptance of what he said. For the notion of ever being a spiritual teacher did not mesh with the contempt and disdain in which I held myself, bound so deeply in bondage to the contraction of personhood.

When I finally acquiesced to see this teacher, a sign of my desperation was the fact that I would have to drive two-and-a-half hours to his satsang, and two-and-a-half to return. A sign of the enduring nature of this desperation was the fact that I would go on to make this drive, one evening a week, for a year and nine months.

A Disappointing Meeting

When the day arrived, I managed to drag myself into my car and make the drive, against fierce inner resistance. Before the satsang I

An Affair of the Heart

met my friend and two of his friends at a natural foods restaurant. As usual when my pundit friend was present, a lively spiritual discussion ensued, full of laughter, often lapsing into respectful irreverence toward various aspects of the whole spiritual affair. I was so happy to see my friend after a long period of isolation, and to meet new friends with whom I would go on to have heartfelt relationships. It had been so long since I'd enjoyed myself as much. After a great meal, I grudgingly followed my friend to the teacher's apartment.

I entered and saw the teacher sitting on a couch at the far end of the living room, smiling in greeting. Several others were sitting around the room, meditating. Why, I wondered, after all that had transpired in my life, had I chosen to once again subject myself to this lunacy. Was the desperate need to get out of the house worth putting up with this nonsense? Not wanting to outwardly display my inner cynicism and sarcasm, I found a chair in the back of the room, closed my eyes, and rested within. I could not bring myself to look at the teacher.

I wasn't there to have a spiritual experience of any kind. At this point in my life, none of that meant anything to me. I was there because my pundit friend had said this teacher was an embodiment of Divine Mother. I was there on a gamble that it was so, and that through the embodiment of Unconditional Love, this teacher might be able to offer some help in resolving the terrible pain of selfhood that plagued me. And if this teacher was not such an embodiment, I stood nothing to lose by spending a few hours resting within, once a week, for an as yet undetermined stretch.

When I did open my eyes I saw no Light and felt no emanation coming from the teacher. I kept closing my eyes, embarrassed at

The Third Teacher of Significance

even being there. When I closed my eyes, however, I noticed, as time passed, waves of the Inner Radiance beginning to wash over my heart with increasing intensity. This was not the powerful tsunami of energy I'd felt emanating from my first teacher, or the softer but powerful emanation of my second teacher. There was no apparent "outer" energy touching me. It was simply a matter of The Inner Radiance welling up powerfully within. The intensity became so great, The Inner Radiance coming in waves with each out-breath, that in time I was simply awash, immersed. Whereas when I'd first walked in I hadn't wanted to take an in-breath due to depression, now I wanted to breath in because with each out-breath the wave of The Inner Radiance's Ecstasy washed over me, and I wanted nothing more than to drown in the Ocean that awaited me at the end of each out-breath.

Eventually the time came for people to ask questions of the teacher. Several questions were asked of him, and I listened and watched with a sour bitterness, having heard those same questions asked again and again over the decades. I was afraid to even try to articulate my dilemma and feelings to him, and in spite of the experience of The Inner Radiance washing over me with such uncommon intensity, I remained skeptical of him.

Finally, I couldn't help myself, and raised my hand, not to ask a question, but to express my exasperation with the whole spiritual affair. I started out clearly enough, like the first few streams of water escaping a dam. But in no time any sense of propriety crumbled, and the dam burst. I poured out my heart, using words I didn't intend, and making little sense, even to myself. If I'd not been on the brink of insanity, I'd simply have screamed, "Help!"

His answers only made matters worse, for he asked how close I

 An Affair of the Heart

wanted to get to him, and later urged me to give all of my suffering to him. Such self-elevated arrogance, I thought. I didn't want to get close to him or any guru. And the statement of giving him my suffering only raised a more serious red flag, causing me to recoil even more deeply. I didn't like this guy.

When I got home, although I'd slept only four hours the night before, I was up for quite some time, wide awake, wondering about all that had occurred. For the millionth time I asked myself, what did it all mean? Although I was confused by the experience of such deep Ecstasy, in the end seeing the teacher had only deepened the well of despair. Here was yet another teacher in whose presence The Inner Radiance welled up in Affinity, but who exhibited, yet again, signs of profound egoity.

An Unexpected Aftermath

But… when I awoke after only a few hours of sleep, my heart was exploding with waves of The Inner Radiance, again, with each out-breath. Only, these waves were even more uncommonly Ecstatic than the night before; what I can only call spiritually orgasmic. My body was "beyond relaxed." It was as if I was deeply asleep, yet awake and alert. When I stretched, my whole body felt Exquisitely Sublime. At the end of each stretch, I felt as if I was melting away, dissolving into an Ocean of Bliss. I barely had it in me to eventually lift myself out of bed. And when I did, the movement was Exquisite.

My wife had gone off to work, and I spent most of the day in bed, more awash in The Inner Radiance than I'd ever experienced, short of the Absolute Ecstasy of Nonexistent Existence. I only had to see the book on Ramakrishna on my night table and I would feel the

The Third Teacher of Significance

instantaneous wave surge up. Not a dramatic, crashing shore-break, but a huge, slow rolling, mid-ocean wave that rolled through the whole of my being.

I tried to sit formally in meditation at one point, thinking to take advantage of this Grace. But as usual with me when I tried to "meditate", The Inner Radiance diminished. When I gave up and laid down again, grateful not to have to exert the energy to hold myself sitting up, I would again be awash. As the week wore on, The Inner Radiance subsided to its "normal" Presence. I'd expected it would, just as it had in the days following meditations with any emanation teacher. This experience gave me the impetus to make the drive the following week. But such an Immersion in Ecstasy never occurred again in relationship with this teacher, during or after satsangs.

Several years later I would go on to experience this strange one-time explosion of The Inner Radiance with another teacher. And I wondered if perhaps such uncommonly profound one-time experiences indicated a past-life relationship, arising in recognition of that relationship, and encapsulating in that singular experience the full scope of that relationship, indicating that no further relationship was needed. But what seemed to the heart to be intuition was quickly dismissed by the mind as mere supposition.

When I mentioned all of this to Baba, and said that I might continue to see this teacher, he again questioned why I would go see teachers, asserted to the contrary, but then added that if I must continue to see this man, "He will need you as much as you need him."

An Affair of the Heart

A Year and Nine Months

Week after week for a year and nine months I dragged myself out to the car to make that journey each Tuesday evening. I eventually found a job, and made the drive straight from work. Many times I sat in my car before starting the engine, snarling out loud in bitter disdain at what I was doing.

Although initially the satsangs were more or less tolerated as the cost of getting out of the house and seeing spiritual friends, eventually, in spite of his claims of being an enlightened master and avatar, I came to feel a kind affection and friendship with this teacher. He exhibited kindness and compassion toward me, and in spite of his grandiose claims, behaved with humility and, I would say, even a childlike innocence. He was tolerant of my spiritual state, never admonishing me to be otherwise than the imbalanced nutcase I'd become at that point in my life.

In that regard I was quite "difficult" in a variety of ways, often speaking my mind brashly during satsangs, and behaving in ways that in relationship with other teachers would have felt like a terrible breach of spiritual etiquette. But with a friend, you can say such things and behave in such ways. His kind-heartedness compensated for the several aspects of this teaching that would otherwise have sent me running. He knew how I felt about Guru Yoga, and told me, early on, not to think of him as a guru, as that would surely send me fleeing.

Fairly soon after starting to see this teacher, I took on the redesign and maintenance of his web site. Through that task I interacted with him far more than others who attended his satsangs, and the friendship only deepened. And looking back over journal entries, I

The Third Teacher of Significance

see that during our relationship I had a profoundly deep gratitude for this teacher's presence in my life.

Another aspect of our relationship that had a profound impact on me was the unique teaching this man presented. We were so closely aligned in how we related to The Great Mystery that during his talks it was as if I was hearing my own teaching being spoken. Things were articulated that were precisely as I felt them with my heart and understood them with my mind, but had never yet articulated to myself. I felt then, and still feel, that certain of his brief talks during that period could replace volumes of words on a bookshelf.

A Sudden Shocking Turn

It was only because of the humility and devotional nature this teacher exhibited that I was able to overlook his claims of being an enlightened master and avatar; statements I don't recall him making overtly during satsangs. He was, during that time[59], although still "the teacher", more like a friend not just to me, but to all of us.

But in the ninth month of the second year, seemingly out of nowhere, he began saying things that startled and troubled me; things that were deeply incongruous with the nature of the person I had come to know.

In the first instance of this, I was blindsided to hear him relate the story of a man from whom he had rented an apartment, and who had then evicted him in an unkind way. This man had subsequently been injured seriously in a car accident; the clear implication

---

[59] When I met him several years after our spiritual relationship ended, he said that the earlier period I had witnessed was, "A rare time of deep bhakti."

An Affair of the Heart

being that this was a consequence of having evicted the teacher. Removing any doubt about this, the teacher went on to add that he wasn't through with the man. And later, still, in the conversation he said, "You don't want to make me mad."

I wasn't simply startled, but in the instant of hearing such words, was brokenhearted. Such statements were, in my experience with this teacher, utterly out of character. A so-called "enlightened master" teaching petty, mean-spirited vindictiveness, and the harming of those who somehow offend him? With these utterances, our spiritual relationship essentially came to an end. I lingered for a few more satsangs, during which time I wrote the teacher about this instance, and received what was, for me, an unsatisfactory response.

Shortly after I noticed the turn in the nature of the teacher, in the last satsang I attended, a remarkable meditation occurred, which I describe in the chapter "The Dam Bursts". But even after our spiritual relationship ended, I continued to have – and have to this day – an affection for him as a friend, and gratitude for the time we'd spent together, during which he'd not exhibited the troubling characteristics that only later appeared.

A few years later I would attend another of his satsangs, hoping the man and teacher I had known in our early association had perhaps returned. But after a break during the satsang, he came out from his bedroom flossing, and on the way to his chair, handed the used floss to an attendee, stating it was prasad. After sitting down, he went on to say that if he allowed it, there were "devotees" who would drink his toilet water. And so it seemed the situation had only gotten worse over time. Still, spiritual dissonance aside, I wish him well, and remember with friendly affection our time together.

The Third Teacher of Significance

Yet again it had been shown to me that the ability to meditate deeply and emanate spiritual energy did not, necessarily, mean that upon returning from the dissolution of meditation, the "person" of the emanator was perfected across all levels of being. In fact, that person could be severely wounded, even broken, in various aspects of being.

 # An Affair of the Heart

The Dam Bursts

*No God was spared,
A lifetime's built up wrath.*

After the heartbreaking remarks and turn of character by my third teacher, and his failure to provide a meaningful response to my query about his comments, the time quickly came for my last satsang with him, in which I intended to say goodbye in person. As I entered the satsang, although feeling deeply disheartened and uncomfortable, I felt nothing unusual, energetically. It seemed to me to be simply another satsang. I quickly took a seat, as always in the back of the room, and immediately closed my eyes. I felt far too uncomfortable to look at the teacher, or risk engaging in conversation with him before the end of the meeting when I planned to formally take my leave.

But from the moment I closed my eyes, something began to come over me, at first slowly, then building in intensity. I realized fairly quickly that what was happening was uncommonly intense, and energetically different than my "normal" meditative experience. It was not simply the result of resting Attention into The Inner Radiance. Something else was going on, almost as if it was happening "to" me. And I soon realized that the flood tide that was quickly turning

 An Affair of the Heart

into a tsunami was... Rage; Rage born of a lifetime of frustrated seeking; not simply my disappointment in this particular teacher. And at some point, an inner dam that had been holding back and moderating this Ocean of Frustration and Rage for all of my life, burst.

In an experience I had never known before, and which is near-impossible to explain, The Inner Radiance Itself seemed to take on the quality of Rage, became inseparable from it, and exploded within me so powerfully that I wondered someone might see the subtle shaking of my body as the raging flood roiled through me. As the experience deepened, it was as if I was experiencing nearly a samadhi of Frustration and Rage, for my awareness came close to being wholly absorbed and vanishing in it.

But it was not samadhi, for thoughts did remain, and they turned to the sacrosanct notion of Divine Mother that I'd held to, white-knuckled, in the face of all disillusionment and discouragement. And for the first time in my life... I unleashed my Rage upon Her, realizing, as I did so, the profound nature, for me, of such an act.

Decades earlier, just prior to the inner enquiry that led to the Experience of Nonexistent Existence, I had cursed the notion of God, religion, and one-by-one, all of the prophets and saints I was familiar with. But back then, at the end of that litany of curses, thinking of Divine Mother, I had held back my wrath, crying out plaintively, instead, "How can you be so cruel?!" Now, for the first time in this life, I let fall that restraint and propriety.

When my thought turned to Her, The Inner Radiance of Rage, as if it had been waiting with fierce anticipation for that thought, intensified even more, and an even fuller Fury was unleashed at

The Dam Bursts

Her. I struck out at Her, energetically, and felt the Current of Rage increase. In that state, I felt that if I had had all of Eternity to beat Her with the full Fury of that Rage, it would not have been long enough. This ferocious energetic attack lasted through the entire satsang. In those moments She had become the imagined embodiment of The Great Suffering and my desperate but fruitless lifelong struggle to be free of it. I had no idea what was said by the teacher, what questions were asked and answered. At the end of the satsang, as I heard chairs moving, the inner Tsunami washed me onto the shore of outer awareness, exhausted, the Rage subsiding, toward God, "enlightenment", and the whole spiritual affair.

Stunned by the strangeness and intensity of what had happened, without saying goodbye to the teacher or my friends, I left the satsang and walked out to my car. I stood there with the door open, gazing up at the stars. I felt… transparent, formless, and light, as if a palpable, visceral weight had been removed from my subtle and somatic bodies; clear, clean, and fresh, as I had never felt in my life. There was no residue of rage, frustration, and… the contraction of seeking. And I Knew that it was over. I was done with the whole affair.

It was not that I had at last succeeded. I had not attained enlightenment or awakening. Nor had I perfected the lesser aspects of my being. Rather, it was a Profound Surrendering to things as they are, to myself as I was, enlightened or not, perfected or not; a great out-breath, across the whole of my Being, of Acceptance. Only one thing had changed; for standing there, the "problem" with it all had Vanished. There was no trace of spiritual dilemma to be found in The Field of Awareness, where it had resided as a part of me, an aspect of me, from my earliest remembrance.

An Affair of the Heart

I could sense that this was not the transient result of a spiritual tantrum. In my spiritual life I had thrown countless tantrums. But I had never felt this before. I was through, and could never turn back, for an energetic contraction, an unease and dissatisfaction in my deepest interiority had simply vanished, leaving no trace. And I asked myself out loud, "What are you going to do now?"

Standing there, I didn't realize that however profound and wonderful the Liberation from seeking felt in that moment, the full depth and breadth of what had happened would not reveal itself for a week or so, when I would suddenly come to an even more startling revelation.

I Can't Feel Charles!

What if, in time, the Radiance in your Heart,
Like a Wellspring of Transmuting Love,
Vanquished the terrible pain of yourself,
Leaving intact all that you had taken yourself to be,
But stealing from your experience, the felt sense of "you",
That very felt sense that had vanished that fateful day,
So long ago in time, when time and all things Vanished...

In the Rapture of Nonexistent Existence.

I knew, when I first started writing this book, that this would be the most difficult chapter to write. For it's near impossible to describe what happened in May of 2003, only a week or so after the dam burst at the last satsang with my third teacher. That said, I'll do my best, and beg forgiveness from the reader.

The Uneasy Fear of Farewell

In the days following the last satsang with my third teacher I was struggling with how I would tell him that I was breaking off my spiritual relationship with him, and why. I'd left the satsang hurriedly,

 An Affair of the Heart

in a kind of shock over the dam bursting meditation, slipping out while everyone was milling about, and not speaking with him as I'd planned to do.

In a strange twist of fate, I found out the following week that he had cancelled satsangs and announced, to the great surprise of his students, that he was taking time off from teaching. I later discovered that a crisis of some sort had arisen between him and someone I had always assumed was his main guru. Whatever had happened, it had evidently shaken him dramatically.

The nature of the relationship with my third teacher had always been one of friendship. And I felt that we had become close spiritual friends. We'd had so many discussions about various aspects of spirituality, and unlike so many teachers who remain aloof and inaccessible, he'd been generous with his time. Part of that may have had to do with the fact that I'd created and managed his web site. And consequently, there were frequent emails and phone calls. This spiritual intimacy only added to the unease I felt about the call I needed to make, in which I'd say goodbye. And so, in spite of the recent change in his nature, and the transmutation that had occurred during that last meditation, I put off calling him, again and again. I couldn't know at the time that this troubling prospect would be taken out of my hands.

The Phone Call

A week or so after my last satsang and the teacher's announcement of suspending teaching, the phone rang. It was the teacher. My heart and stomach sank simultaneously. The moment of truth had come. He said, "Mother told me to call you." When I asked why, he said, "She didn't say." This took me aback, but somehow comforted me.

I Can't Feel Charles!

For the announcement I had to make would not simply be coming from me, but in the context of his statement, would be coming from Mother.

I don't recall how the segue happened, but in fairly short order I launched into a tirade about the whole spiritual affair. It was as if the Rage I'd felt inwardly at the last satsang welled up again and found verbal expression. As I ramped up, almost shouting, I Raged against the notion of enlightenment and all of the suffering it engendered; far more, in my experience, than the suffering it was supposed to alleviate. I cursed the Gods and Goddesses, and so-called enlightened gurus, giving special wrath to the many corruptions I'd seen. I used language one wouldn't use, even in the company of close friends. As I Raged, I paced from room to room, near breathless, for there was barely a gap between my sentences. It was an unstoppable and continuous flood of Frustration and Rage.

At some point I ran out of breath, and coming to my senses, shouted, "What are we supposed to do?!" "Yes, what are we supposed to do?" he replied, sympathetically. Realizing, suddenly, what I had just spent so many minutes doing, how horribly inappropriate and crude my language had been, I said, "I'm sorry, you don't need to be subjected to this. I better go." But he said, "She won't let me go."

I should note that I wasn't really sorry at all, but simply saw how inappropriate it was to subject a friend to my lunacy. Regarding all I'd said, I felt it was all absolutely true, but simply stated in a manic, unhinged, and shockingly crude manner.

And again, I don't remember how I segued, but somehow, again, I rejoined my tirade. And I paced, and paced, from room to room, again breathlessly Raging. Until once again, out of breath, I paused and again said, "Look, I'm really sorry. I better go." But again he

An Affair of the Heart

responded, "She still won't let me go."

And again, a third time – I understand this seems unimaginable – I allowed myself to indulge, unhinged, in Frustration and Rage, pacing the house, breathlessly ranting. Until, exhausted, I found myself standing in the laundry room, out of breath, unable to go on any longer. In that pause, before I could say anything, he said, "There it is. Transmission." And knowing how I despised the superiority so often implied in such statements by teachers of the emanation paths, he added, "Not transmission from me to you. Just transmission." After a pause in which I didn't respond, he said, "She'll let me go now." We said our goodbyes and I hung up the phone. I don't believe I ever told him I was leaving the spiritual relationship with him.

Normally, after having ranted like an out of control lunatic, shouting obscenities and curses to God, gurus, and the whole spiritual affair, even to a close friend, much less a man who had been my teacher, I would have hung up and immediately felt heart-dropping, gut-wrenching embarrassment, shame, and regret. For the things I'd said, and the way I'd said them could never be taken back. Instead, as if nothing at all embarrassing or trauma-inducing had happened, I walked casually and calmly from the laundry room into my bedroom, laid down on my bed, turned on the tv and watched a football game briefly. Then I channel surfed to figure skating; then to a movie; then a news commentary; then back to football. I opened the window behind me and felt the breeze enter the room. It was as if I'd simply forgotten or had transient amnesia of all that had just transpired, as if it hadn't happened at all. In fact, I recall feeling relaxed and at peace.

And then…

I Can't Feel Charles!

Laying there, relaxed, watching the game, feeling the breeze through the open window... I suddenly awakened with a start from my amnesia, and remembered, in a flash, all that had transpired; all that I had said, and the unrestrained way in which I had said it. In the instant of remembering, I sat up in bed. And in that instant of sitting up, instead of gut-wrenching, heart-sinking embarrassment, psychological horror, and the onset of nausea, I realized with a subtle shock and perplexity that there was none of that within me; not a trace of reactivity in the Field of Perception. And in what I can only call a calm startlement, a far more unbelievable realization occurred. For in addition to their not being any reactivity in the Field of Perception, for the first time in my living memory... I could not feel my personal self[60], within; I could not feel Charles.

I was sitting there, existing, *without* the felt sense of Charles, the person, and all of the mental, psychological, emotional, energetic, and somatic aspects of moment-to-moment experience that had comprised the feeling of him. They were all gone. Further, where the contraction of Charles had been felt in the Field of Perception there was... a Serene Emptiness. I felt the breeze from the open window moving *through* me, not upon "me"; the breeze unobstructed by a tangible object that had formerly existed across so many levels of being.

---

[60] For my best take at describing what I mean by the personal self, see the chapter, "On Having Become Someone". My hope is that it will give you some notion of what it was that had vanished.

An Affair of the Heart

The Metaphor of the Library

Imagine the felt sense of our personal self as a library. Initially the shelves are empty, and the clean, fresh air of the room is enhanced with the rich fragrance of our wood, of our Essence. One by one, books are added to the shelves. Each book is an experience had during our life, its pages containing qualities and attributes; moments of pleasure and pain, embarrassment and exaltation, praise and blame – any from among the vast possibilities of attribution. Each book contributes to our sense of self-image-identity-worth, and how we feel about ourself as a consequence of the experiences. Each book creates, as well, a subtle, or not so subtle, conditioning; a psycho-emotional reactivity to such situations or circumstances that becomes, over time, habituated, reflexive, and mindless, arising prior event to thoughts about the situation or circumstance.

When there are only a few books on the shelves, we can remember the specific experiences contained in each book, feel the reactivity created from those memories, and, more importantly, how we feel about ourself as a consequence of those experiences. But as time passes and more and more books accumulate, we find ourself unable to recall the contents of all but the most recently added books. And yet – and this is *so* important – the conditionings from the earlier books remain, as vague and amorphous aspects of our increasingly solidified self-image-identity, and as silent, unseen contributors to how we feel about ourself. Although no longer specifically remembered, their presence is felt as a quality in the air in the library, in the feeling of the room. And in time, the initially fresh, clean air and the rich fragrance of wood becomes overpowered by the musty smell of countless old books whose contents are long forgotten, but whose impacts remain.

I Can't Feel Charles!

Just so, the felt sense of Charles had come into being. And just so, sitting up in bed this day, I found the library burned to the ground, many books consumed in the flames, many laying in the open air, charred, more so or less; intact… but now… unhoused, unowned.

What was it that Vanished?

My body remained; my mind remained; my preferences, propensities, and proclivities remained; my memory remained; I still answered to my name; the knowledge I'd acquired over a lifetime remained; the sense of experiencing subjective awareness through this particular Vehicle of Perception remained. Countless other aspects of existence as a manifest Being remained. I still called all of these things "mine", for they applied to me, not you. I saw through my eyes, not yours, and heard through my ears, not yours. And today, I am sitting here writing, while you are not. All of these things remained, but unowned, belonging to no one. Only the felt sense of Charles had vanished from the Field of Perception, from my manifest Being.

A "Condition", not an Object

The felt sense of Charles had not been, in fact, the felt sense of an object, but rather that of a *condition*, only mistakenly taken to be a self-existent thing that was alive. When we're infected with a virus, we can point to specific aspects of our experience – headache, nausea, aches and pains in specific parts of our body – but there is also that vague, amorphous sense of illness that's difficult to pinpoint and define. Even so was the felt sense of Charles; the experience of a condition that had given rise to the felt sense of its existence as

 An Affair of the Heart

an object, a "thing" that was alive, qualified by characteristics and attributes, good and bad, desirable and undesirable, pleasant and unpleasant.

The inner mechanism that had created that condition had stopped.

The Mechanism/Engine of "Person"-Generation

The virus that had created this condition was a "person"-generating *mechanism*; an ongoing process of self-concern, self-reflection, self-assessment, self-qualification, self-judgment, and the feeling, born of a lifetime of this mechanism's functioning, of "me" as an object-perceiver-experiencer-person to whom all of that self-referencing referred. But more importantly, it was the resulting feeling "about" myself, the esteem or lack thereof, born of that self-referencing. And it was so much more that I'm simply unable to differentiate or articulate, even to myself.

It was this mechanism, this process that had stopped, and with it, the felt sense of Charles that the mechanism had long ago created and then perpetuated. The product of the mechanism – the imagined perception of, and the palpable and visceral sensation of Charles – had vanished from the Field of Perception. Instead of the incessant energetic whirring of the person-generating machine, there was Silence and Stillness. Instead of the felt sense generated by that machine, only Serene Emptiness.

The Effects

At the level of psychology and emotion, the engine of personhood had created a continuous feeling of inherent insecurity, unease, and

I Can't Feel Charles!

anxiety. The prime directive of that engine was a relentless concern over stature, in all aspects of personhood.

At the subtle-energetic level it had instilled a contraction that was more subtly sensed than overtly felt. This contraction was so closely interwoven into both the psychological and somatic aspects of Being as to be indistinguishable, until, that is, it vanished. Only then did its former existence became apparent through its absence.

But most stubbornly, there had been created *a somatic contraction*. After Nonexistent Existence, the intellectual sense of an individuated self had been shattered, functioning only notionally. But on the somatic level of Being, more so even than on the subtle-energetic, a stubborn contraction endured. This somatic contraction had been more immediately and acutely felt as a density. It was that sense, more than any other, that was noticeable in its vanishing that day. However much the mind may have *Known* that I was more than simply an object-perceiver-experiencer-person, and however profound the impact of that Knowing, the body had continued to *feel* the dense residues of contraction.

All of these effects had ceased.

A Quality of Nonexistent Existence, Present in Manifest Existence

I had discovered on the Journey to The Kingdom of Heaven[61] that the contraction of personhood, of Charles, was not native, but acquired, having accrued over time. That contraction had vanished

---

[61] See the chapter, "The Journey to The Kingdom of Heaven".

   An Affair of the Heart

in the Experience of Nonexistent Existence, but had returned with the first subtle emergence, from Nonexistent Existence, of subjective awareness. But now… here… in manifest existence, that contraction was gone.

I sat there stunned, unbelieving even in the face of my direct experience. For nothing I had done over the decades since Nonexistent Existence had rid me of the pain of the personal self. All those years of the salt doll self immersed in the Ocean of The Inner Radiance had not rid me of it; all those teachers, all of those experiences, all of those tearful sobs, all of those enraged tantrums.

I had reached a point of such unbearable Frustration and crushing Despair, and had lived in that condition for so long that the last vestiges of hope had long been extinguished.

Had all of that played a role in what had happened that day? Countless questions would arise over time. And for most of those questions, to this day, I have no answers. But I strongly suspect that the salt doll, having drifted for so long like detritus immersed in the Ocean of The Inner Radiance, had finally Dissolved, if not completely so, to the point where only a shapeless residue remained; apparitional, no longer perceptible in the Field of Awareness.

I did not become a perfected being. I simply ceased to feel, within my manifest being, Charles, the person; the Intercessor Self. The "person" who experienced everything from this point on – the Charles who answered to his name – was perceived outwardly to be a person, but existed inwardly only in a "notional" sense. This Vanishing of the person was, as a friend put it, a subjective Grace, not necessarily perceivable outwardly. That said, my pundit friend said that he noticed the disappearance from my persona of subtle evidences of the spiritual frustration and bitterness that had previously been present.

Divine Mother Laughs

It was no doubt my imagination, but the image suddenly appeared in my mind of Divine Mother as a little girl – I'd never imagined Her that way – sitting in lotus posture, off to my right, clapping Her hands and laughing so gleefully that She fell over backwards, continuing to laugh and clap. Imagined or not, a wave of unbridled celebration rippled through my being, and for the first time a happy smile broke through the bewilderment that had been my expression since sitting up.

The Dispersion of The Inner Radiance

There was another aspect of this experience. For as I sat there, I realized that The Inner Radiance, which, since the Experience of Nonexistent Existence, had always had its locus in my heart, and which in the previous year or so had become a veritable Ocean of Bliss, had dispersed into a soft, gentle ambience, everywhere, in all things; unseen, but present. It still glimmered in my Heart, but not with its former intensity. This dispersion only increased the sense of Emptiness that I felt. This might otherwise have been a bit troubling, but in my Joy at having been freed from bondage to the personal self, I only took note of this dispersion, then moved on, continuing in celebration.

 An Affair of the Heart

The Word "Liberation"

To simplify expression, from this point forward in this book I'll refer to this transmutation as liberation. I understand that that's a lofty-sounding word, and don't mean to confuse it with its use in various traditions, where its definition is in fact quite lofty. But in the context of my experience – again, not to be confused with "moksha" or other such terms – it's a suitable term. To make the term less lofty, I will not initial-capitalize the word. But I was in fact liberated from terrible, hopeless bondage to the felt sense of the personal self.

The Great Suffering had lost one of its elements, and was reduced to The Great Sorrow and Existential Fear. For I continued to feel sorrow at the suffering inherent in this world, and continued to feel existential fear during certain circumstances. But neither was experienced any longer by an Intercessor self.

Emptiness Deepens

A Great Hollowing Out,
Where it seemed nothing remained,
To be hollowed.

A Period of Intense Upwellings

In the days and weeks after sitting up in bed I began to experience extremely dramatic upheavals of emotions and states of mind; moments of sorrow, anger, horror, despair, even desolation; often so intense I felt I couldn't bear them. They arose seemingly out of nowhere, without apparent cause, endured briefly – often only a few minutes – with breathtaking intensity, then vanished instantly, leaving no trace whatsoever.

Normally, after experiencing these sorts of intense emotional traumas, the impact would linger for hours or days, slowly diminishing from the initial intensity, but leaving a lingering residue, like the smoke and soot from a powerful blast. But now, their near instantaneous vanishing left no residue, as if absolutely nothing at all had happened.

The best example of these arisings is the first instance, that occurred

An Affair of the Heart

when I was watching a movie one evening and decided to make some tea. I got up from the couch and began walking around the large island in my kitchen. When I was half-way around the island, I looked up at the clock and noted the time. Suddenly I became overwhelmed by the most intense heartache. I felt as if someone had committed the most terrible romantic betrayal. Before I reached the stove, I was sobbing. It was unbearably painful, and I thought back to times in my life when I had felt such heartache and had wondered at my ability to bear the pain and continue existing. I made the tea, drowning the whole time in this heart-wrenching agony. I picked up the cup and began walking back to the couch. Half-way around the island on my return trip I glanced up at the clock and noted that five minutes had passed. And in that instant I realized, as well, that the unbearable heartbreak had vanished, utterly, with not a trace of it to be found in the Field of Perception. No residue *whatsoever*.

That experience shook me. And when other such experiences followed in the weeks to come, involving other emotions and states of mind, I actually became fearful, and wondered that I might need "professional" help. For their intensity, as in the first instance, was near unbearable, and their instantaneous disappearance, without leaving a trace, was just… not normal. Fortunately, the incidences diminished over six months or so, and stopped by the end of the first year.

But there was a dramatic difference from previous experiences of intense emotions or states of mind, beyond the confounding fact of their instantaneous arrival and vanishing. After the experience that occurred when I sat up in bed, when these incidents occurred, they were experienced as simply the movement of energy, a natural occurrence; the effects of innumerable causes, long lost to memory,

Emptiness Deepens

in a life that was an endless stream of causes and effects; each effect, in turn, a cause; and on and on.

> Like a rock breaking apart from a cliff,
> After eons of sun, wind, and rain,
> And rolling down a hill.
>
> Like wind blowing through the trees
> Causing them to sway,
> And producing a rustling.
>
> Like water flowing,
> Carrying leaves and twigs along,
> Producing a gurgling song.
>
> Like heat rising off the pavement,
> In a shimmering mirage,
> On a hot summer day.

Emptiness Will Deepen

Not long after these experiences began to happen, I called Baba to explain the experience of liberation, and the experiences that were happening afterward. He said that these arising were the results of samskaras and vasanas. The sense I got from the conversation was that they were like chunks falling off of an iceberg – the iceberg being latent residues of the contraction of personal-identity. But that is not fact; only the sense I got. Another image was of the salt doll self, no longer recognizable as a self, but still existing as chunks of salt, still in the process of dissolving. He said that in Hinduism these incidents were born of what was called "prarabdha karmas"; deep-seated residues that were "under the hood", so to speak, no

 An Affair of the Heart

longer plaguing us as aspects of personal-identity and our ongoing experience. But make no mistake, he cautioned, they were still there.

When I told him that in place of the contraction of self-identity that I used to feel, there was now only Serene Emptiness, he said something that left me confused and uncomfortable; "Emptiness will deepen. Then will come power." Power? What did he mean? I didn't want power. I wanted to be a Blessing. I'd seen "powerful" teachers before, and they'd all been wounded humans, some even horribly broken. In my mind at that time, power, as I understood it, had become somewhat of a negative. The odd thing is that in that moment, I didn't ask him what he meant. I was focused on the first part of his statement. How could Emptiness deepen? It seemed to me that there was nothing there, nothing left to deepen where "I" had been felt.

In the two years following liberation, I would come to see the fulfillment of what Baba said, and his prediction was startlingly accurate. Also, in the end, I would come to understand what he meant by power.

Emptiness Deepens

In the days, weeks, and months that followed liberation I often searched inwardly, checking whether the contraction of the personal self had returned. And to my disbelieving amazement, it had not. I had expected liberation might be yet another transient state of being. But it proved to be a station[62] arrived at.

---

[62] In Sufism, enduring transmutations are called "stations". There are many stations along The Way.

Emptiness Deepens

As time passed, and the incidents of samskaric upwelling diminished, I actually became accustomed to existence without the contraction of self-identity. This experience of being became quite... normal, but in a way, of course, I'd not experienced previously. I might be sitting on the couch watching a movie and suddenly, recognizing the normalcy of my experience, wonder, "Did anything really happen when I sat up in bed that day?" Then I would check within, and sure enough... "he" was gone, nowhere to be found.

The dispersion of The Inner Radiance no doubt played a part in this perception of normalcy. Its previous intensity had been a constant reminder that my ongoing experience was anything but normal, whereas now it existed only as a soft ambient background, barely discernible unless I searched for it, within. There were rare moments when it welled up, the cause often unknown. But as time passed, it seemed as if it might actually be dimming more and more.

I also noticed, as Baba had said, that as the glimmer of The Inner Radiance slowly dimmed, I began to feel myself Emptier and Emptier. And as Emptiness deepened, it became less and less Serene and more and more like a great hollowing out... and troubling.

 An Affair of the Heart

Little Monkey

The most Exquisitely Sweet Emanation

The name of the teacher in this story isn't Little Monkey. Well, it is, and it isn't. One of his teachers, a Chinese-Tibetan woman, felt his Indian name was too lofty and potentially ego-inflating, so she called him Little Monkey. I also spent a brief period in relationship with this woman, and she called me Shiao Dai. I could never get a clear rendering of what that name meant. Shiao means little, or younger, but Dai remained a confusion. The closest I could come to understanding the meaning of Shiao Dai was "Little Idiot" (Idiot in the eyes of the world, but not in what she called "Dharma Eyes").

A "Nature Walk"

On Sunday, February 8th, 2004, against my better instincts, I found myself driving to Topanga Canyon to see the latest guru du jour that my friends were fascinated with. This was no contemporary nondualist – a Westernized form of nonduality had been all the rage on the spiritual scene for some time. Although a Westerner, I'd been told this teacher was as Hindu as they come. He had supposedly spent

 An Affair of the Heart

time in India in some rather austere traditional Hindu sadhana[63]. Rumor had it that he'd actually spent time meditating in an ice cave in the Himalayas. I dismissed this as probably being exaggeration and mythologizing. But a year or so later a photographer student of the Chinese-Tibetan woman declared that while he had been traveling through India, he'd actually run into Little Monkey, and in an ice cave. You just never know.

A friend had emailed me earlier in the week about a "nature walk" with Little Monkey that was taking place that Sunday. She warned me that he was eccentric, to put it mildly, but that there was the most powerful, and profoundly beautiful spiritual energy about him. Setting aside my cynicism, feeling the need to get out of the house, and looking forward to seeing my friend, I told her I might show up.

The Strange Vanishing of The Inner Radiance

Although after liberation The Inner Radiance had become an ever more subtle ambience, it had never left me completely. So I was startled, confused, and deeply troubled when I awoke the Sunday of the nature walk to find that any trace, whatsoever, of The Inner Radiance was gone. This had not happened in all of the years since its advent. It was a terrible feeling. For no reason that I could fathom, I'd suddenly become as I had been before the Experience of Nonexistent Existence. I felt dense, embodied, and energetically flat; flatter, it seemed, than I remembered ever feeling, even before the advent of The Inner Radiance.

Equally startling and horrifying, I felt the contraction of selfhood. It

---
[63] The journey of one's spiritual seeking and, usually, referring to the practices engaged in.

Little Monkey

had returned, even more densely felt than I remembered it before Nonexistent Existence. In a state of dumbfounded perplexity, I decided, nonetheless, to drive to LA, as it wouldn't do any good to sit at home and wonder what on earth was going on.

On the drive, I wondered if playing my favorite spiritual music might ignite the now ashen Inner Radiance. Song after song that often brought me to tears had no effect; no effect whatsoever. The situation grew increasingly confounding. What was happening, and why? The sense of embodied density was so very painful, and the inner aridity almost sickening.

As I drove on, I suddenly felt ridiculous about making the drive to Los Angeles to see a spiritual teacher. I had not yet learned of him as Little Monkey, and my friends had spoken of him using his lofty Indian name. Considering his name, my lip curled in cynicism and disdain, for skepticism had only deepened over the years. None the less, and oddly so, given my cynical state, The question arose as to what spiritual name I would take if I was so inclined, and could choose one. At the arising of that thought, cynicism rolled through me even more powerfully, and I dismissed the question outright, again crinkling my nose and curling my lip.

Vishnu

At last my favorite spiritual song at that time came on; George Harrison's "My Sweet Lord". Incredibly, in this state, even this song meant less than nothing to me; no inner response whatsoever. Indeed, there was no longer an Inner Radiance that might respond. I thought of turning around at the next off ramp, and going home. Then, near the end of the song came the refrain, "Guru Brahma,

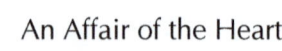 An Affair of the Heart

Guru Vishnu." And in the instant of hearing the word "Vishnu" I burst instantly into gasping, sobbing tears. I couldn't breathe, I was crying so hard. But this insane intensity lasted only a few seconds, for as that word passed and the song continued... almost as quickly as the tears had come... they vanished, as did their accompanying emotions, and I returned to the desert state of dense, energetically flat, embodied selfhood. This utterly strange event had happened "to" me.

I had no idea what to make of this, and thought, as I had so often over the years, that I was certifiably crazy. Why had the word Vishnu transported me from the Desert of the human condition into the deepest depths of the Ocean of Love and Longing? And why in God's name had I then been transported back to that Desert?

I found the location where my friend said everyone would be meeting. We were to park outside the park, stay in our cars, and then drive into the park as a group. Her car was the first in the long queue parked along the side of the road. I parked several cars behind her. I hope I've made it clear that I was not in the mood for this. And sitting there, I wished more than ever I had turned around and driven home.

Then something caught my eye. Through the sunroof of her car, a man was standing, waving a samurai sword, then pointing it to the entrance to the park. Her car pulled into the park entrance and we all followed; a veritable caravan. As she drove off, the man remained in the open sunroof, waving the sword, admonishing everyone onward. When we entered the park, people walking by the side of the road were startled and frightened by the lunatic waving a sword, and wondered at the long string of cars. I felt embarrassed to be a part of it, and pondered turning around and going home, no matter

Little Monkey

how rude it might be. This was ridiculous.

We parked. My friend's car, with the teacher, was several cars further up the road. As I got out of my car, I saw the teacher running along the line of cars, toward me. He ran up to me, excited, even a bit frantic, and standing uncomfortably close said, "You are Vishnu! You are Vishnu! And more! Much more! May I call you Vishnu?!"

What?! Vishnu. That name. The response to that name on the drive up; that momentary tsunami of Tearful Rapture, vanishing as quickly as it had come. What was I to make of this? I spent the rest of the day in mind-stopping shock.

At one point during the hike we ambled up a steep hillside. I'm terribly afraid of heights, and nearing the top, the path we'd been traversing became too narrow for my comfort, with what seemed to me a precipitous drop if one mis-stepped. The path turned sharply at this slim point, and my fear increased by not being able to see around the turn. Suddenly an arm appeared around the turn, and I heard, "Come Vishnu! I'm your Garuda[64]!"

No, I don't for a minute think that I'm an incarnation of Vishnu, or any such nonsense. And no, I did not take Vishnu as a spiritual name. But to this day, my reaction to the word Vishnu has been transmuted, and it seems to me the Most Beautiful of words, the hearing of it often bringing tears for no apparent reason, causing The Inner Radiance to well up powerfully.

Why had The Inner Radiance vanished inexplicably that morning? Why had it suddenly exploded in my Heart at hearing the name "Vishnu", only to vanish in the instant of that words passing? Why

---
[64] In Hindu mythology, the mount of Vishnu.

 An Affair of the Heart

had someone I'd never met before – and a crazed lunatic at that – run up to me after all of that, exclaiming excitedly, "You are Vishnu!"? What did all of this mean?

I suddenly remembered the Vision of Vishnu and Lakshmi, and became even more shocked and confused.

Even to my fiercely empirical mind, the string of events that day seemed to have been volitional, purposeful, occurring so the name would stand out even to one as thick-headed as I am, in dramatically stark contrast to the terrible nature of experience that had surrounded the hearing of that name. I certainly hadn't done any of that. But who or what could or would manipulate manifestation like that? And to what end? And all conjecture aside, what was my relationship to that name? The question remains unanswered.

But I have to say that if spiritual names are "given", this one was given by The Great Mystery itself.

The Sweetest Ecstasy

After that crazy "nature walk" I saw Little Monkey one more time that's of note. During the walk, I hadn't noticed any spiritual energy from him. In fact, I'd remained in the uncommonly flat state until some point on the drive home, when The Inner Radiance slowly returned to its dimmed ambience, and the contraction of selfhood diminished, and at some point vanished. When my Los Angeles friend called to tell me Little Monkey would be at the house of one of her friends the next afternoon, I remained uninspired, even after all that had happened. That said, again, just wanting to get out of the house, wanting to see my friend again, and also curious about

Little Monkey

this strange fellow and all that had happened, I drove up the next day.

Several folks were sitting in a back room, waiting for him to arrive. I sat down, feeling awkward and uneasy. When he arrived, he sat next to me. He spoke briefly, then asked one of the people there to describe Buddhism for everyone. He'd heard this person was well educated on spirituality, and eloquent. The person proceeded to give one of the worst descriptions of Buddhism I'd ever heard, and wanting to escape, I turned my head slightly, away from the speaker and those gathered, so as not to be conspicuous, and closed my eyes. To my surprise, The Inner Radiance welled up unexpectedly, and so powerfully that I felt myself on the brink of Absolute Dissolution. As it welled up, I turned my head a bit more, not wanting to "pray in public", as the Bible says.

The Quality of The Inner Radiance was different than I'd felt before with any teacher; of the deepest, most profound, most Exquisitely Beautiful Bhakti[65]. I was barely breathing. In that Dissolution, I lost all concern for how I might be appearing to others. Later I would realize that my face was lifted upward in Rapture. Then, in the midst of that Dissolution-Rapture, I felt something touch my lip. Mustering my will against the Gravitational Pull of The Inner Radiance, I cracked my eyes open ever so slightly and saw that Little Monkey, ignoring the lecture on Buddhism, was holding a slice of tangerine to my lips.

Again, mustering will against the Gravity of Ecstatic Dissolution, I took it, and closed my eyes, sinking again into the Depths. Again, after a time, another slice. And then, after a time, something different;

---

[65] In Hinduism, the feeling of Love and Devotion for The Divine.

 An Affair of the Heart

he was holding a bottle of water to my lips. I took it, and again sunk back into the Sweetest Embrace of The Beloved.

Remembering the Experience later, it felt like what I had always imagined it would be like to have been with Ramakrishna.

You might find it odd that I did not see him again. But in spite of all I've described, the desire simply was not there, even though, to this day, I have a tender spiritual affection for him.

The Sorrows of the World Pour In

The Suffering of the world,
Pours into the Emptiness,
Where "I" had been.

I can't remember exactly when it began happening, but at some point around the end of the first year after liberation, after the intense samskaric arisings had subsided, The Great Sorrow began to well up within me; no longer so much the aspect of rage, as an exhausted sorrow at the suffering of the world. It began slowly at first, then increased, filling the Emptiness that would continue to deepen over the course of the next year. The trickle became a stream, a river, a lake, a sea, until finally it felt like an Ocean of Sorrow, within.

After liberation The Great Sorrow hadn't left me, but had simply been pushed, briefly, into the periphery of Awareness by the jubilation I had initially felt, before Emptiness ceased being Serene, and came to be felt as a great hollowing out. The more Emptiness deepened, the more Sorrow flooded in, filling the void. And as the second year unfolded, I found myself crying more often and more deeply than ever before in my life regarding the nature of existence in form.

I understood, in the midst of this period, that my experience and

An Affair of the Heart

view of life, predominated increasingly by The Great Sorrow, was skewed and irrational. Sorrow is, of course, not the totality of life. The Beauty of life is as unimaginably wonderful as the Horror is terrible. But something was going on; something I couldn't understand. For some reason – and at the risk of sounding woo-woo I'll say that I feel it was Mystical – my inner experience was being *held* in this state; heart and mind held under water, subjected to this period of drowning in The Great Sorrow.

I suspect a Mystical cause because, when this state eventually ended, it would certainly seem as if there had been a purpose; not a terrible purpose, as it seemed through most of the year, but a Beautiful purpose, only revealed at the end. That said, during the Deepening and Inpouring, I felt nothing but confusion and despair. None of my prayers for clarification and an end of Sorrow were answered, and I felt abandoned and desolate.

The hallmark of this period was a completely irrational Desire that possessed me; a Desire that flew in the face of reality, the hopelessness of which broke my heart:

> All suffering must cease,
> Now,
> Everywhere,
> And forever.

As the waves of this Desire broke again and again against the rocks of reality, I became ever more distraught, ever more exhausted. For the Desire was fierce, and would hear nothing of compromise.

The following instances are indicative of this period.

The Sorrows of the World Pour In

The Tree

On my drive to work there was a tree that I found particularly beautiful. Driving past it one day, awareness of the transience of manifest existence overwhelmed me, and I burst into tears of Love and Compassion for the tree, with which I shared this transient existence. But woven into the fabric of this Love and Compassion was a heartbreaking Sorrow for the inevitable suffering of the tree as it grew old, struggled, and died. And I found myself sobbing, overwhelmed with the prayer that it not suffer in its passing; that no living form, anywhere, ever suffer.

I understand that all of this sounds insane. And as I had during the intense welling up of samskaras during the first year after liberation, I wondered at my sanity. But it made no difference that I had no certainty that trees might suffer. Such logic was irrelevant. My heart was broken, and there was no reasoning with it, no holding back the onslaught of The Great Sorrow. It was wholly irrational, and I was unable to stop it.

At Work

At work, I would walk down a corridor of cubicles and see the weary, bored, stressed, often sorrowful faces of so many. And questioning the existence of a Merciful God, I would take the power of Blessing upon myself, saying, inwardly, with a touch of defiance, "If you do not exist to Bless, then *I* will do it!" And as I passed those cubicles I would whisper, within, "God Bless you, dear. God Bless you, sweet heart. Mercy. Mercy. Grace." I would sometimes have to struggle to hold back tears. Throughout the day, wherever I might be, I would see the faces of so many who were simply wrapt in the

An Affair of the Heart

"human condition" – whether well-adjusted within it, or in pain – and have to fight back the Sorrow and tears.

Out and About

I stopped once to buy coffee, and noticed how uncommonly beautiful the young girl was, behind the counter. And it struck me, probably based on my own experience as a man, that she would likely be loved by men who were drawn to her, first and foremost, by her beauty. After all, I had only been in romantic relationship with those I found attractive, and in my youth, that attraction had often played a predominant role. And as had happened with the tree, the span of her life flashed before me, and I saw an old woman looking back on a life in which conditional love had perhaps danced predominantly, a life in which she may have experienced heartbreak born of conditional love. But included in my concern for her was the broader scope of life's sorrows; losing loved ones, experiencing periods of terrible existential fear, or any of the sorrows that befall us as humans. And as before, against all logic and reason, as I drove away I began sobbing, not simply for the girl, but for everyone. Like the tree I drove by each day, she was an embodiment, an icon of a broader scope. I prayed that her lovers be those in whom a deeper Love shared residence with desire and conditional attraction.

The Fleeing Mother

But the most iconic instance, and most recurring, was the image in my mind of a woman fleeing some terror or other. Her head was covered in a shawl, and she carried a baby in her arms. She was looking backward, over her shoulder, in terrible fear at what

The Sorrows of the World Pour In

lay behind. And again, against all rationality and reason, simply seeing this imagined image in my mind, I would begin sobbing, unable to bear the knowledge that in every moment of every day, such imagined images were real, somewhere on this earth. Such images… and worse.

The Prayer

In each of these cases, and so many others, my wish, the Blessing I prayed for, was not simply that everyone and everything experience the transient happiness that comes from condition and circumstance, but that the Heart of their Being be Filled with The Inner Radiance, a Radiance that had become only a faint distant glimmer now, in my own Experience. I prayed that it Shine in their Hearts more brightly than it had ever Shone in mine, and that if they came to that greater Illumination, they would turn, hold out their hand, and help me.

In those moments when I held this overwhelmingly powerful intention to Bless, The Inner Radiance did well up, but only briefly, soon receding to its distant glimmering, as if pulled there, or pushed to the periphery of experience by a force unseen.

 An Affair of the Heart

The Reason to Live

This is Not the Heart's Desire

As 2005, the second year after liberation unfolded, I became conflicted about liberation. If it had caused this Deepening, this Inpouring of Sorrow, and this dispersion of The Inner Radiance, was it worth it?

Although an Unimaginable Blessing, liberation was not, in itself, the Fullness of The Heart's Desire, but only one aspect.

All of my life I had longed not only for the ending of the pain of selfhood, but for the advent of The Inner Radiance. And so, the equanimity I had felt immediately after liberation regarding the dispersion of The Inner Radiance had soon vanished, and I found myself mourning that dispersion, and even more so, its continuing diminishment.

But the nature of The Inner Radiance is such that it is not something you can track down, grasp, and hold on to[66]. Although it was,

---

[66] Since The Inner Radiance first Illumined my Heart, I have always had an intuitive sense, powerfully felt, that it is inappropriate to grasp after it. Such grasping felt somehow crass and sorrowful; like groping The Beloved.

An Affair of the Heart

to me, the Ecstasy of my formless Essence Shining into manifest experience, that Shining into manifest experience was apparently subject to conditionality. For prior to liberation, The Inner Radiance had Shone with breathtaking Brightness, and after, had dispersed and then continually dimmed.

Hinduism's notion of Soul-obscuring samskaras and vasanas came to mind, as well as Sufism's notion of obscuring veils. Had liberation somehow caused the re-emergence of veils thought previously to have been removed or made transparent enough for The Inner Radiance to Shine into manifest experience? My mind spun in such considerations and conjecture, while my Heart simply sobbed in despair. But all conjecture and desperate theorizing aside, during this period The Inner Radiance simply did not Shine Radiant and Powerful in my Heart as it had before liberation, and there was nothing I could do to summon it back. It continued to dim, and I feared that it might eventually vanish from my experience altogether.

Something was happening to me. And my prayers expressing confusion and desperation had gone unanswered. I came, eventually, to a place of utter Desolation, wondering if there was any Joy in life, any Beauty sufficient to push out this Sorrow. Why had Emptiness deepened? Why had The Inner Radiance been pushed to the periphery? Why had Sorrow poured in? Why was I helpless in the face of this onslaught? Why was this all happening?

In February, a year and nine months after liberation, one day, exhausted from the whole affair, I walked into my lower living room and sat on the floor in Despair. One by one, I gave consideration to those things that had formerly brought joy in my life; things that might possibly stand as bulwarks against The Great Sorrow that possessed me. But nothing that came into my mind had any impact.

The Reason to Live

Yes, the things that came to mind were Beautiful, and Joyful, and Life Enhancing. But they were recognized merely as memories, distant and dim, garnering no response in the present.

And I wondered, had I simply succumbed to clinical depression; some bio-chemical imbalance? Perhaps there was nothing at all "spiritual" about all that had happened since liberation? Perhaps liberation itself was some strange physiological anomaly that had, in its occurring, done damage elsewhere, somehow?

I didn't bother cursing God or The Great Mystery as I'd done so many times earlier in life. I was too exhausted, and saw no benefit from such flailing. I had sunk too deeply into the Ocean of Sorrows to think rationally or reasonably. In that moment, all the Unimaginable Beauty of creation held no charm against that Ocean. Yet again in my life, I sobbed so deeply I could hardly breath, gasping like a frightened rabbit for breath.

And then, out of nowhere, I saw it…

The Smile

It was an image in my mind, and yet, it felt spatial in the room. It simply appeared. Above me, off to my right… a woman's mouth, smiling. No face or body. Just a mouth, smiling. But not just a smile; a happy smile. One of those smiles on the brink of bursting into laughter. But not just laughter; happy laughter.

Such an image might seem to have nothing to do with what I was thinking in that moment – my desperate attempt, and failure, to find some joy powerful enough to vanquish Sorrow at the suffering

 An Affair of the Heart

of the world. But in the instant of seeing the Mysterious Smiler experiencing a moment of happiness, before any thought could arise in the mind, my Heart Exploded in Compassionate Love for her, and... a Fathomless Happiness and Joy burst within me... at seeing her happy.

In that instant, my tears changed from those of my own subjective Sorrow and Despair, to those of Gratitude that someone, anyone, was experiencing happiness. I was happy... for her. And within this Happiness at the happiness of another, it didn't matter that any of life's tragedies might one day befall her. In this moment of her Happiness, and my Happiness at her Happiness... all of life's sorrows were forgotten... The Great Sorrow was forgotten, removed utterly from experience.

"Yes, sweetheart!" I cried between sobs of Love and Gratitude for her happiness. "You be happy! You be happy, dear!"

And overwhelmed in Love and Happiness for another, I experienced a near-samadhi[67] of Love and Compassion. And when I regained awareness of space and time, the room, and myself sitting there... I knew the reason to live.

The Inner Radiance Floods In

There are no words to describe the emotions I felt when I realized that while I had been taken by Love, unconscious of all else... The Inner Radiance had, after almost two interminable years as a diminished ambience, returned from its hiatus and Filled my Heart.

---

[67] The Absorption of awareness, in this instance, in Love and Compassion.

The Reason to Live

And I hope you'll forgive me for being an insane lunatic, but I cried new tears, yet again; tears of Fathomless Relief, Immeasurable Gratitude, Boundless Appreciation, and perhaps the most Precious gift of that moment… Affection for the fact of existing, and for all that exists.

There were many tears, of many kinds, in this Experience.

> There came a day, some years ago,
> When the world's suffering overcame me,
> And drowning in an Ocean of Sorrow,
> I wondered at a reason to continue.
>
> Finding nothing in the world's enticements,
> I sat sobbing, having lost all hope,
> Until, amidst my tears, there appeared,
> A vision, only of a woman's smile.
>
> No face accompanying, but only a smile,
> A smile not yet broken into laughter,
> But on the brink, near bursting with joy,
> Happiness, there, in the smile of another.
>
> And in that instant, my tears transmuted,
> For without thought, attention turned,
> From myself, and the Ocean of sorrows,
> To Happiness, there, on the face of another.
>
> And the whole of me was Taken, wholly,
> By a Happiness, Pure and Unalloyed,
> A Happiness born of only one cause;
> The Happiness of another.

 An Affair of the Heart

The world Vanished, and I Vanished,
And only Loving Compassion remained,
And tears of an Unbearable Longing,
For the Happiness of the Mysterious Smiler.

When I emerged from Oblivion in Love,
And my eyes perceived, once again,
This world of countless Sorrows,
I had been Shown the reason to exist.

I Revel now, in the enjoyments of this life,
Which before, had lost their savor,
And I cry, still, for the Sorrows of the world,
But constant, now, in both Joy and Sorrow,
Find Life's Greatest Happiness…

In the Happiness of another[68].

Not You!

Later that day, I recalled Baba's prediction, and wondered in amazement at how he'd known that Emptiness would deepen. Who was he? What was he? And then I recalled the second thing he had said; that after Emptiness deepens, "Then comes power." What did he mean by that? If he'd been so startlingly accurate regarding the deepening of Emptiness, there seemed a very real possibility that whatever he meant by "power" would come about. By power, had he meant the Filling of Fully Accomplished Emptiness with The Inner Radiance?

---
[68] Whether "another" be sentient or insentient.

The Reason to Live

The very day after the Experience in the lower living room, a spiritual friend called. Although I knew her from the time with my third teacher – at the time of this call she was still studying with him – our friendship had been fairly casual. In fact, a certain uneasiness, at least on my part, had been an aspect of this relationship from its inception, when my pundit friend had first introduced us. For while chatting casually with her after our introduction, I had, without intending to, said something that offended her, and received a harsh chiding. A coolness persisted between us for some time thereafter, until we eventually became uneasy friends. Only much later would a closeness and friendly affection come about. But that was not yet the case at the time of this call.

I don't remember why she called that day. As usual, though, the discussion turned to the spiritual. After some time she excused herself to get a glass of water. When she returned, she exclaimed with disbelief, "What's going on here?! When I got up to get water, I could hardly walk, I was so Spiritually Intoxicated!" And then she exclaimed, with a mix of that same shock and disbelief, but also a subtle touch of the lingering contempt in which she had held me since our unfortunate introduction, "Not You!"

And so it began.

> What if you were told one day,
> To your surprise and amazement,
> By some among your Friends,
> That the Ember in their Hearts Ignited,
> To their Delight and Inspiration,
> In moments of Relationship with you,
> Shining ever more Brightly, over time…

 An Affair of the Heart

Until they found themselves, in time,
Imbued with The Inner Radiance,
Shining in the Locus of their Heart,
Sometimes the ambient background,
Sometimes flooding the foreground,
Ever available to their mind's Attention,
Ever available to their Heart's Remembrance…

I would call that… a reason to live.

Epilogue

All these words I have written of Illumination and Liberation,
May have given you the illusion that I have my bearings,
And an understanding of all that's happened,
And all that is to unfold over time,
While I am simply adrift,
Without compass,
Rudderless,
Here…

In this Great Mystery.

A Simple Man

This book was written as mere context for the poems on https://gardenofthebeloved.com, which are, far more than this autobiography, the essence of the author's Heart, and will, in time, become a book of their own.